From Sinners to Saints

From Sinners to Saints

A Guide to Understanding the
SACRAMENT OF RECONCILIATION

Kurt Stasiak, OSB

PAULIST PRESS
New York / Mahwah, NJ

The Scripture quotations contained herein are from the New Revised Standard Version: Catholic Edition Copyright © 1989 and 1993, by the Division of Christian Education of the National Council of the Churches of Christ in the United States of America. Used by permission. All rights reserved.

Nihil Obstat: Daniel J. Mahan, STB, STL
Censor Librorum

Imprimatur: Most Reverend Christopher J. Coyne, SLD
Vicar General and Moderator of the Curia
January 3, 2013

Cover image by Jenny Sturm / Shutterstock.com
Cover design by Sharyn Banks
Book design by Lynn Else

Copyright © 2014 by Kurt Stasiak, OSB

All rights reserved. No part of this publication may be reproduced, stored in a retrieval system, or transmitted in any form or by any means, electronic, mechanical, photocopying, recording, scanning, or otherwise, except as permitted under Section 107 or 108 of the 1976 United States Copyright Act, without the prior written permission of the Publisher. Requests to the Publisher for permission should be addressed to the Permissions Department, Paulist Press, 997 Macarthur Boulevard, Mahwah, NJ 07430, (201) 825-7300, fax (201) 825-8345, or online at www.paulistpress.com.

Library of Congress Cataloging-in-Publication Data

Stasiak, Kurt, 1952–
    From sinners to saints : a guide to understanding the sacrament of reconciliation / Kurt Stasiak, OSB.
       pages cm
    Includes bibliographical references.
    ISBN 978-0-8091-4895-0 (pbk. : alk. paper) — ISBN 978-1-58768-418-0 (ebook)
    1. Confession—Catholic Church. 2. Penance—History. 3. Sacraments—Catholic Church—History of doctrines. 4. Reconciliation—Religious aspects—Catholic Church. I. Title.
    BX2260.S73 2014
    264'.02086—dc23
                                                      2014014922

ISBN: 978-0-8091-4895-0 (paperback)
ISBN: 978-1-58768-418-0 (e-book)

Published by Paulist Press
997 Macarthur Boulevard
Mahwah, New Jersey 07430

www.paulistpress.com

Printed and bound in the
United States of America

CONTENTS

Introduction vii

1. The Sacrament 1

2. Celebrating the Sacrament 19

3. Examination of Conscience 35

4. Frequently Asked Questions 51

Epilogue: Hearing Confession 73

Notes 79

Further Resources 85

To Walt and Sue
Kindness to a father shall not be forgotten (Sirach 3:14).

INTRODUCTION

Why this book? For most of the last twenty years, I have taught the course on the sacrament of reconciliation at Saint Meinrad Seminary and School of Theology in southern Indiana. I teach that course to our deacon seminarians, men only a few months away from their ordination to the priesthood. Unlike some of my other courses, I have never had to spend much time during the first class period telling my students how important this course is. They know that. The seminarians know how important the sacrament has been in their lives, and they want to "continue the tradition." They want to be good confessors. They want to be ministers of pardon and peace. They want to be instruments and stewards of God's forgiveness.

Who is this book for? I continue to teach and to write for those who "hear confession," but my focus here is on what I can offer to those "on the other side of the screen." I'm writing this book for those who have questions about the sacrament and, frankly, that seems to include just about everyone! I've spoken to many individuals and parish groups about the sacrament of reconciliation over the years, and I've learned that I always need to leave time for questions. Penitents come in all shapes and sizes. But whatever the shape or the size, the questions are always there.

And so I write to Catholics who are confused about the sacrament. I write to those who feel alienated from the Church. I write to those who have questions about the why's, the what's, and the how's of confession, but don't know how to ask them, or perhaps feel they have no one whom they can ask. I write to those for whom confession is a mystery, a puzzle, a curiosity—or a threat.

I write also to those who do go to confession and do find it helpful. I hope this book will help them celebrate the sacrament even more effectively. As a priest friend of mine is fond of saying, "Most of us aren't great sinners; we're just lousy saints." And so I write to myself and my fellow lousy saints, for we all know that no matter how good we are, we can become better. Finally, I write to those who have joined our Church through the RCIA and perhaps are still perplexed as to the purpose or the method of this distinctively Catholic sacrament of forgiveness.

In the first chapter, I offer several ways of thinking about the sacrament of reconciliation. I discuss the various names for it—confession, penance, reconciliation—and suggest some reasons for going. The next three chapters deal with the actual celebration of the sacrament. Chapter 2 offers a step-by-step guide through its celebration. Chapter 3 offers several examinations of conscience and different tools you may use when preparing for confession. Chapter 4 is the lengthiest one, which addresses questions people frequently have: questions about the sacrament, about the confessor, and about themselves as penitents. And in a brief epilogue, I offer some thoughts on a topic that intrigues many people, Catholic and non-Catholic alike: what is it really like to hear confession?

Throughout this book, I refer to the ritual, or the *Rite of Penance*. Published by the Vatican in 1973, this is "the priest's book." It outlines the basic theology and what the Church teaches about the sacrament of reconciliation, sets forth rules and regulations that govern its practice, and contains resources such as prayers and scripture references for use during its celebration. While the ritual is a valuable resource for both priests and parishioners, I know that my readers usually will not have

Introduction

ready access to it. Some footnotes, therefore, provide the actual text or commentary from the ritual. "Further Resources" provides the Web site from which you can access the entire text of the *Rite of Penance*, as well as other helpful information.

Because the sacrament of reconciliation is often referred to as confession or penance in everyday Catholic life, I use the three terms interchangeably throughout this book. Furthermore, although I sometimes use the terms *penitent* or *parishioner* to refer to those who approach the sacrament, I have tried to write to you, my reader, as directly as possible. That is what I want, most of all: to engage in a discussion, insofar as that is possible here, about the sacrament—how you might want to approach it and, especially, what it can offer you.

I thank the Rt. Rev. Justin DuVall, OSB, Archabbot of Saint Meinrad Archabbey, and the Very Rev. Denis Robinson, OSB, President-Rector of Saint Meinrad Seminary and School of Theology, for allowing me the time to work on this book. I also acknowledge my gratitude to Josh Cole, Brendan Kelly, Scott Lutgring, and Fr. Alan Carter, former students of mine, for their thoughtful review of the manuscript and the suggestions they offered.

Finally, I dedicate this book to two friends, Mr. Walter Mendus of Ocala, Florida, and Ms. Sue Czarnetzky, of Annandale, Virginia. Perhaps they think they might learn something from these pages. If that be true, so be it. I certainly treasure what I have learned from them.

Chapter One
THE SACRAMENT

The 1970 movie *Love Story*, based on Erich Segal's best-selling novel of the same name, is remembered in part because of its last line. Oliver (portrayed by Ryan O'Neal) interrupts his father's expression of sympathy over the death of Oliver's lover with the memorable words, "Love means not ever having to say you're sorry."

Two years later, *What's Up, Doc?* starring Barbara Streisand and, again, Ryan O'Neal, hit the screens. At its conclusion, Ms. Streisand interrupts O'Neal's attempt at an apology as, with eyelashes fluttering, she coos, "Love means never having to say you're sorry." After a poignant pause, O'Neal's character retorts, "That's the dumbest thing I've ever heard!"

I agree with *that* conclusion! Love *does* mean having to say you're sorry. And the deeper the love, the more often "sorry" likely has to be said. For the deeper we love someone, the more we are aware of how the love of that person is a gift—a gift we certainly have not earned, a gift we never fully deserve.

The first thing we can say about God's love for us is that it is a *gift*. We are given the gift, not because we are worthy, not because we have been "good enough," and certainly not because we have earned it. We enjoy the gift simply because God loves us enough to offer it to us. The gift of God's love is free, but it does come with "strings attached." God asks us to *use* his gift by loving him in return and by extending that love to others. We do this as best we can, but we know we often fail. And when we fail, we need to apologize and make amends for the future. Because love *does* mean having to say you're sorry.

Just as it is important for us to ask God for forgiveness—to tell God we are sorry we have offended him—so is it also important for us to hear God's response. One of the seven sacraments of our Catholic Church offers us the unique opportunity to do both: to express our sorrow and to hear God's continuing offer of forgiveness. This unique opportunity goes by different names. In fact, the *Catechism of the Catholic Church*, published in 1994, offers five names for this wonderful opportunity to ask for and receive God's forgiveness. It is the sacrament of *confession*, *penance*, or *reconciliation*. It might also be called the sacrament of *forgiveness*, or the sacrament of *conversion* (*Catechism* 1423-24). So just what is the "real name" of this sacrament?

Each of the five names above is correct, for each tells us something about a particular aspect of the sacrament. For example, many Catholics say they are "going to *confession*." This traditional name emphasizes a particular act of the sacramental celebration: the acknowledging of one's sins to a priest.

The sacrament is also traditionally referred to as *penance*. In fact, *Rite of Penance* is the title of the book containing the bible texts, prayers, and instructions, and that serves as a resource to priests in celebrating the sacrament. The name *penance* reminds us of another important aspect about the sacrament: that we not only confess our sins but, by offering some kind of satisfaction, we also try to repair the damage or ease the hurt we have caused through those sins.

Then there is *reconciliation*, the preferred name of the sacrament for many since the early 1970s, when the *Rite of Penance* was revised according to the directives of the Second Vatican Council (1962-65). A New Testament term, *reconciliation*, refers to the effect, the result of the sacrament: God, through his loving mercy, reconciles—calls sinners back—to himself.

The Sacrament

Finally, referring to *confession* as the sacrament of *forgiveness* or *conversion* suggests two additional aspects of the sacrament: that "by the priest's sacramental absolution God grants the penitent 'pardon and peace,'" and that confession "makes sacramentally present Jesus' call to conversion, the first step in returning to the Father from whom one has strayed by sin" (*Catechism* 1423–24).

WHAT'S IN A NAME?

That the sacrament goes by several names reflects the fact that people celebrate the sacrament for different reasons, with different attitudes, and even with different hopes or intentions. Again, each name is correct and appropriate, but perhaps the most important name is the word which applies to all of the above terms, the word *sacrament*.

A traditional definition of *sacrament* is that it is a "visible sign instituted by Christ that gives grace." Another way of defining a sacrament is to understand it as a time of prayerful celebration through which we encounter the invisible God in a visible and tangible way. To say that confession (or penance or reconciliation) is a sacrament of God's mercy is to say that the celebration of the sacrament not only *reminds* us of our belief and hope in God's mercy, but also—through the words of the prayer and through the presence and ministry of the priest—*expresses* that belief in a way we can better experience and so believe and appreciate it. Confession, penance, or reconciliation is a *sacrament*.

> For God so loved the world that he sent his only Son, so that everyone who believes in him may not perish but may have eternal life. Indeed, God did not send the Son into the world to condemn the world, but in order that the world might be saved through him. (John 3:16–17)

Whatever name it goes by, the sacrament of reconciliation continues the work of Jesus Christ by giving us the opportunity to acknowledge our sins and hear the gracious words of God's forgiveness. Our Catholic Church is a sacramental Church. We believe that the saving work of Christ continues to be made present to us, continues to be made effective for us, through the signs and symbols of the liturgical celebration, and through the words of faith proclaimed by the Church's ministers. This understanding of sacrament is one reason why, as Catholics, we confess our sins to a priest.

For where two or three are gathered in my name, I am there among them (Matt 18:20). We believe Christ is always present to us. The problem, however, is that many times *we find it difficult to be present to him*. The words, gestures, and symbols that make up our sacramental celebrations can help us with that difficulty. They place us in Christ's presence in such a way that we can more clearly experience, more firmly believe in his saving action. The sacrament spares us from having to rely on mere wishful thinking or a desperate hope that God responds to our sinfulness as a "Father of mercies." God doesn't need the sacrament, but we do. We need it because God's words and actions are spoken and shown to us through the person and ministry of the priest, who stands and acts in the person and in the name of Christ.

WHY GO TO THIS SACRAMENT?

Many people have different reasons for *not* going to confession. Some may not really know what the sacrament offers. Others may have had an unpleasant experience. Others, understandably, feel shame and guilt about what they have done and find it difficult to admit their sins to another. It seems that a good number of people who were brought into the Church as adults were never taught the question the Church has tried to address from her very beginning: as powerful as the sacrament of baptism is, what do we do when we find ourselves still failing in our Christian duties and responsibilities after baptism? Here, I want to consider some reasons why celebrating this sacrament is worth your while. Some of the reasons are obvious, for example, so that sins will be forgiven. Others are perhaps more subtle.

Why go to confession? The most obvious answer is that there are times when we *need* to go. That word *need* has several meanings. For example, the Church teaches that we need to celebrate the sacrament—that we are *required* to go to confession—when we realize we have committed a grave (mortal) sin. What is a "mortal" sin? We'll discuss that below. But first, in a more general sense, we often hear that the world has lost a sense of what sin is. That may be true to some extent but, given the ways things are today, the world has certainly not lost its ability to sin!

WHAT IS SIN?

Sin can be defined in many ways. Simply put, sin is anything—an action, a thought, a word, a failure to act or speak—that offends God and harms others. Sin offends God *and* harms others. This is an important point. Jesus said there are *two* great commandments. We cannot separate the two, nor can we choose to obey one and ignore the other:

> One of the scribes…asked him, "Which commandment is the first of all?" Jesus answered, "The first is, 'Hear, O Israel: the Lord our God, the Lord is one; you shall love the Lord your God with all your heart, and with all your soul, and with all your mind, and with all your strength.' The second is this, 'You shall love your neighbor as yourself.' There is no other commandment greater than these." (Mark 12:28–31)

Saint John leaves no doubt about the relationship these two great commandments have to each other:

> Those who say, "I love God," and hate their brothers or sisters, are liars; for those who do not love a brother or sister whom they have seen, cannot love God whom they have not seen. The commandment we have from him is this: those who love God must love their brothers and sisters also. (1 John 4:20–21)

Sin is not a private affair, a matter just between me and God. This is another reason we ask for forgiveness through a sacrament of the Church. Our sin offends God and harms others, and so we ask and receive forgiveness both from God and from others. As the *Catechism* reminds us:

> Those who approach the sacrament of Penance obtain pardon from God's mercy for the offense committed against him, and are, at the same time, reconciled with the Church which they have wounded by their sins and which by charity, by example, and by prayer labors for their conversion. (1422)[1]

Some might well ask, "How can we, mere humans, offend a God who is all-powerful and almighty?" It's a good question. To help us answer it, recall my comments on the two movies with which we introduced this chapter. God is all-powerful; God is almighty. But as we concentrate on these impressive qualities of God, we at times forget another of God's great attributes. God is all *loving*. And where there is love—where there is someone who loves—there is always the possibility of refusing that love, or of not returning the love in due measure.

Just as catechisms offer various definitions of sin, so does the Bible present us with different images or accounts of sin. In the first dozen chapters of the Book of Genesis we find accounts of three basic types of sin.

Disobedience toward God

God created us in his image. When we sin we are trying to fashion our own gods in our own image. We're familiar with the Bible's account of Adam and Eve. God presented all his creation to them to enjoy. He asked only that they not eat the fruit of a particular tree. But Adam and Eve reached out and grabbed what God had not meant for them to have. This is what the Church calls *original sin* and, to make a play on words, this "original sin" was just that: Adam and Eve forgot their "origins." They forgot from whom they came and for whom they were made. They acted as though they were the masters of their own destiny and so had a right to whatever they wanted, whenever they wanted it.

Hurts Our Neighbor

God saw it was not good for man to be alone. Yet when we hurt our neighbor—our brother or sister in Christ—we are acting as though we are the only person who really matters. Adam and Eve's original sin was not only contagious, it mutated into an especially deadly form. Let's review the story of their two sons, Cain and Abel.

> Now Abel was a keeper of sheep, and Cain a tiller of the ground.
> In the course of time Cain brought to the LORD an offering of the fruit of the ground, and Abel for his part brought of the firstlings of his flock, their fat portions. And the LORD had regard for Abel and his offering, but for Cain and his offering he had no regard. So Cain was very angry, and his countenance fell.

> The LORD said to Cain, "Why are you angry, and why has your countenance fallen? If you do well, will you not be accepted? And if you do not do well, sin is lurking at the door; its desire is for you, but you must master it."
>
> Cain said to his brother Abel, "Let us go out to the field." And when they were in the field, Cain rose up against his brother Abel and killed him.
>
> Then the LORD said to Cain, "Where is your brother Abel?" He said, "I do not know; am I my brother's keeper?" And the LORD said, "What have you done? Listen; your brother's blood is crying out to me from the ground! And now you are cursed from the ground, which has opened its mouth to receive your brother's blood from your hand. When you till the ground, it will no longer yield to you its strength; you will be a fugitive and a wanderer on the earth." (Gen 4:2–12)

Cain, the firstborn son of Adam and Eve, kills his brother, which leads God to ask, for the second time in those first few years of human history, "What is this you have done?" Along with this evil side Cain picked up from his parents, he inherited also a share of their punishment, for God expelled him from his field, dooming him to be a "fugitive and wanderer" upon the earth. It's not difficult to sense God's disappointment and frustration that part of his creation seems to have "gone wrong."

Keeping Out God

To ignore someone we love is to love a lot less than we should. A few chapters after the sad account of Cain and Abel, Genesis reports a sin far more subtle—and more common. The incident with the tower builders of Babel may not be as well known as the sin of Adam and Eve, so let's consider the full account.

The Sacrament

Now the whole earth had one language and the same words. And as they migrated from the east, they came upon a plain in the land of Shinar and settled there. And they said to one another, "Come, let us make bricks, and burn them thoroughly." And they had brick for stone, and bitumen for mortar. Then they said, "Come, let us build ourselves a city, and a tower with its top in the heavens, and let us make a name for ourselves; otherwise we shall be scattered abroad upon the face of the whole earth." The LORD came down to see the city and the tower, which mortals had built. And the LORD said, "Look, they are one people, and they have all one language; and this is only the beginning of what they will do; nothing that they propose to do will now be impossible for them. Come, let us go down, and confuse their language there, so that they will not understand one another's speech." So the LORD scattered them abroad from there over the face of all the earth, and they left off building the city. Therefore it was called Babel, because there the LORD confused the language of all the earth; and from there the LORD scattered them abroad over the face of all the earth. (Gen 11:1–9)

The intentions of the tower builders of Babel were certainly understandable. They wanted to "build [themselves] a city...and make a name for [themselves] (Genesis 11:4). But they became so preoccupied with themselves and their project, they had neither time nor room for the one who gave them the bricks with which to build. Saint John Paul II made an interesting comment about the tower builders. He said their sin was not so much a fighting against God as it was "of forgetfulness and indifference towards him, as if God were of no relevance in the sphere of man's joint projects" (*Reconciliation and Penance* 14).

These three accounts from the Book of Genesis help us understand what sin is and what it does. Sin is a violation of the law of God (Adam and Eve). Sin is inflicting harm on our neighbor (Cain). And sometimes sin is simply our allowing ourselves to get so carried away by our work, our plans, and our desires, that we get carried away from God (the tower builders of Babel).

Not all sins are equally serious, of course. Traditional Catholic teaching speaks of sins that are *mortal* and those that are *venial*.

If we understand *grace* as a measure of our relationship with God, then being in a *state of grace* (another traditional Catholic term) means we are responding to God's invitation to love him by worshipping him and by being charitable to those with whom we live and work. Remember, "love God *and* love your neighbor" are the great commandments. But what do we mean, really, by being in a state of grace?

Basically, being in a state of grace means being in a "right relationship" with God. How do we measure our relationships? Consider what we say. We *like* this person. We *love* that friend. We are *in love* with our spouse. We measure our relationships according to their depth: how much this person means to us, how much we mean to them. How much does God love us? Enough to send his only Son into our world to die for our sins! How much do we love God? Whatever the answer, we can always add, as we can when talking about any loving relationship, "we can always love more."

Being in a state of grace compared to being in a state of physical health can help us better understand the difference between mortal and venial sin. All sins damage our body (and here we can think of our membership in the Body of Christ, the Church). Some sins cause minor pains, temporary upsets. They weaken our overall health, although even with them we can continue to live in a state of grace—a state of "spiritual health"—and continue to contribute constructively to building up the body (of

Christ). These are the sins we call *venial* sins. They are the everyday, ordinary sins. Like germs, bacteria, and viruses, we'll never rid ourselves of them entirely. They weaken us, but they don't kill us. But just as it is with physical disease, there are sins that are more serious, sins that are deadly.

MORTAL SIN

The *Catechism* defines *mortal sin* as a sin that "destroys charity in the heart of man by a grave violation of God's law" (1855). Perhaps some concrete examples of these grave violations of God's law will be helpful in understanding what mortal sin is, and later distinguishing these kinds of sins from what the Church considers venial sins.

In the first few centuries after Jesus, the Church considered the gravest sins to be murder, adultery, and apostasy.[2] We will leave apostasy aside, since those reading this book likely do not consider themselves outside the Church! It is clear why the Church attached such gravity—such "grave matter"—to murder and adultery. Murder is as clear a violation of the commandment to love one's neighbor as can be had. And adultery is a betrayal of the most intimate expression of love between spouses.

But there are other ways we can "destroy charity…by a grave violation of God's law" and so sin in a mortal way. To deliberately, willfully, and seriously damage the reputation of another is certainly a grave sin against charity. So is placing another's life or resources in jeopardy by deceit or malice. When one takes an oath to tell the truth and then lies, the courts call that perjury. The Church calls it a grave (mortal) sin, because we are invoking God as a witness in a serious matter about which we have lied. Deliberate cruelty in word or deed that breaks a person's spirit and does them serious spiritual, psychological, or physical harm is certainly a grave offense against charity. So is obvious indifference to a situation of injustice or jeopardy suffered by another, especially if there are helpful things we could have said or practical remedies we could have offered.

The above examples, of course, are not a complete list of mortal sins, and no such list could ever be drawn up. But they should give us a better idea of what kinds of words, actions, and omissions the Church considers to be a "grave matter"—and why.[3]

"Requirements" for a Mortal Sin

According to Church teaching, three conditions must be present at the same time for a sin to be considered mortal. First, the action (or lack thereof) must be grave. I've indicated above what some of those actions and omissions might be.

For a sin to be considered mortal, we must also be fully aware of its gravity or seriousness. In other words, we must know that what we are doing is a serious violation of the commandments of God. Some might see this as a bit of a loophole, since it would seem to allow ignorance or an uninformed conscience to always let us off the moral hook. ("I'm no professional religious, I just live here!") But this is not so. Each of us has the duty to reflect on the commandments of God and the teachings of the Church and to have a reasonably clear idea of what is required of us and what is forbidden. There is no great mystery here, for we believe that the essential principles of the moral law—in our context, a "Christ-like attitude and behavior"—are a very part of our being human. We find some evidence of this in that parents instinctively recognize and assume as one of their primary duties teaching their children how to distinguish right from wrong.

A third condition that constitutes a mortal sin is that we act with full freedom and consent. If we are forced to do something, or if we act out of extreme fear, what we do may be an objectively grave wrong, but we are not guilty of a mortal sin. For example, if an unmarried pregnant teenager wants to give her baby up for adoption but her parents force her to have an abortion, then she is not the one who commits the mortal sin. If a business associate blackmails a colleague into stealing large sums of money, it is he, and not the colleague, who stands guilty. Faced with such extreme situations, we must do all in our power to extricate ourselves from the difficult circumstances. But if we cannot, we are not guilty of mortal sin. Mortal sin is not something that "just happens," or something we "accidentally fall into," and it is certainly not something we do against our will. It is a serious action we choose knowingly, deliberately, and willingly.

VENIAL SIN

The Church teaches that "individual and integral confession and absolution constitute the only ordinary means by which a member of the faithful conscious of grave sin is reconciled with God and the Church" (*Code of Canon Law* 960).[4] But the Church also knows that the sacrament heals different people in different ways:

> Just as the wounds of sin are varied and multiple in the life of individuals and of the community, so too the healing that penance provides is varied. Those who by grave sin have withdrawn from communion with God in love are called back in the sacrament of penance to the life they have lost. And those who, experiencing their weakness daily, fall into venial sins draw strength from a repeated celebration of penance to reach the full freedom of the children of God. (*Rite of Penance* 7)

We may not be grievous sinners, but none of us is perfect. Ordinarily, we don't set out to hurt others, but we know that many times we do just that, thoughtlessly and carelessly. In our better moments, we say we want to love God and grow closer to him, but so many times we keep him far from our minds and our hearts (recall the sin of the tower builders of Babel). Taking the time to recall our venial sins and confessing them encourages us to get back on track, to remind ourselves that we can do something about the way we live. Seen in this way, the sacrament of reconciliation can be one of the ordinary means that supports our everyday efforts to become better Christians. While it is not *required*, "the regular confession of our venial sins helps us form our conscience, fight against evil tendencies, let ourselves be healed by Christ and progress in the life of the Spirit" (*Catechism* 1458).

CONCLUSION

The primary reason for going to confession, of course, is to receive and be assured of God's forgiveness for the sins we have confessed. But the sacrament can be something more, and for many people it is. After all, we see our physicians not only to try to fix or take care of something that has gone wrong, but also to learn how to stay healthy and enjoy even better health. So, too, celebrating the sacrament of reconciliation provides an opportunity for us, not only to repent of our sins, but also to grow in grace and virtue, and to commit ourselves to a practice of spiritual health. When speaking about our spiritual life and health, again an analogy with our physical life and health may help us understand this important point. One way we care for our bodies is through good habits, such as a healthy diet and regular exercise. To be spiritually healthy takes work—and workouts—as well. The sacrament of reconciliation can be a regular part of a Catholic's *spiritual exercise*.

Spiritual *exercise* leads to spiritual *health*, and, in the context of this chapter, it means growing ever more into a relation-

The Sacrament

ship with God in and through Christ. Relationships need work; they need practice. Relationships grow by trial and error, by love offered, received, and returned. The sacrament of reconciliation offers us the opportunity to reflect on the love God has offered us, and gives us the time and reason to fill in the blanks with our words and actions the "movie cues" that began this chapter: "Love (of God and others) means _____."

Nor should we underestimate the "accountability factor" the sacrament of reconciliation offers us. Left to ourselves, we tend to do less than we can, not as much as we should. Holding ourselves accountable to another is a great help in working on our conversion. We've lived with different forms of accountability all our lives. Homework, tests, papers, and projects helped us to be accountable when we were students. Many jobs today come with standards by which we can measure our actual performance in light of our goals and our company's expectations. In much the same way, the sacrament of reconciliation can provide us with an opportunity to take account of how well we are mastering the business of our Christian conversion.

Some people have said they don't bother going to confession because it doesn't seem to make any difference in their lives. They confess the same sins time and again, and know they will commit them next week and the week after that. "Why bother trying to fix it if it keeps breaking?" they ask. Once again, a comparison with our physical health may help here. There are times when no amount of doctoring, no dosage of medicine, may solve or "fix" what is wrong with our bodies. We may never cure our diabetes. Most likely, we'll never be able to throw away our glasses or contact lenses. And allergy season will always have us sneezing and blowing our nose.

These conditions can't be "fixed," but they can be *managed*. In a similar way, the opportunities confession affords—our taking account of our sins, our refusing to give up, the wise and helpful counsel our confessor offers, the support and possibly the remedy a penance can provide—can assist us in managing our conversion of life. Confession may not solve a specific problem. But it can be one of the steps we take in managing, and living with, a difficult situation or annoying habit more effectively.

There are times when we might be pleasantly surprised. We know our sins, but we really do not know how someone will react to them. Most of the time, far better than we think! In my own confessions (as a penitent), I have often benefited from a comment my confessor has made. Usually this is neither a profound insight nor a life-changing directive, but a simple comment that clearly reflects my confessor's understanding of, and care for, me. It's the experience I often think of as the "grace of being surprised by God's presence." God does talk to us in our prayers, but he also talks to us through other people, especially when we and those other people find ourselves together in the context of prayer.

Baptism is the sacrament through which "we are freed from sin and reborn as sons of God" (*Catechism* 1213), and so some people think that there is no need for, or value of, an additional sacrament of forgiveness. Although baptism has made us "holy and without blemish" (Eph 1:4; 5:27), we know well that it doesn't take much time before we begin to soil and stain—and sometimes even tear—those new clothes of Christ we have put on. An analogy with marriage may help here. A husband and wife exchange their vows of marriage once. But the meaning and the practice of those vows—what they promise and what they require—must be renewed constantly if the marriage is to grow and flourish. Ideally, the love between the spouses will never be in question, though experience suggests otherwise. But even if the love is always there, "acts of contrition" in the marriage are necessary for the continual making and realization of that love. Baptism and marriage are about establishing a relationship and growing in that relationship. And in every relationship, reconciliation is a constant and necessary companion.

The Sacrament

Finally, some people, when they hear the word *confession*, think immediately of their sins and their act of confessing them. That's understandable for, as we know, the confessing of our sins is an essential part of the sacramental celebration and experience. The word *confession*, however, has another meaning.

> It is called the *sacrament of confession*, since the disclosure or confession of sins to a priest is an essential element of this sacrament. In a profound sense it is also a "confession"—acknowledgment and praise—of the holiness of God and of his mercy toward sinful man. (*Catechism* 1424)

Confession is an act of thanksgiving! When we celebrate the sacrament, we do confess our sins, but we also confess our belief in and our gratitude to "God, the Father of Mercies, who through the death and resurrection of his Son has reconciled the world to himself and sent the Holy Spirit among us for the forgiveness of sins."[5]

In the next chapter, we will consider further the Church's teaching concerning the sacrament of reconciliation, and will also proceed step-by-step through the celebration of the sacrament itself.

Chapter Two

CELEBRATING THE SACRAMENT

In the previous chapter, we discussed several aspects of the Church's teaching on the sacrament of reconciliation. In this chapter, we consider the procedures and the mechanics, the nuts and bolts if you will, of celebrating the sacrament.

The first point is that there really is no "wrong way" to go to confession. The celebration of the sacrament won't come to a grinding halt if you are confused about what you should do next, if you can't remember the words of a certain prayer, or even if you forget to confess something. The priest is there not only to hear your confession but also to help you experience the sacrament and the grace it offers in as calm and reverent a manner as possible. Be reassured, priests do not expect, nor will they demand, that everyone confess in exactly the same manner, using exactly the same words.

THE FOUR PARTS OF THE SACRAMENT OF RECONCILIATION

There are four essential "parts" or building blocks to the sacrament of reconciliation, three of which involve an attitude, an acknowledgment, or an action on the part of the penitent. These are *contrition*, the actual *confession* of sins, and the *act of penance*. The *Rite of Penance* remarks that these parts that belong to the penitent "are of the greatest importance," and that they "become part of the sacrament itself, which is completed when the words of absolution are spoken by the minister in the name of Christ" (11).

Contrition

The *Catechism of the Catholic Church*, to which we referred in the previous chapter, defines contrition as "sorrow of the soul and detestation for the sin committed, together with the resolution not to sin again," and considers that "among the penitent's acts contrition occupies first place" (1451).

Priests assume that someone coming to confession brings contrition with them. They do not have to listen long or particularly hard to hear someone express, directly or indirectly, that they are disappointed in themselves: disappointed for not following the Golden Rule; for not acting or speaking as they should have; for finding it difficult to forgive or ask for forgiveness or, as a friend once expressed it, "for just doing dumb things."

Those who come to confession because they know they have sinned should take some comfort in the knowledge that their very coming to the sacrament is itself an indication that God's grace is already acting within them. It's not as though God is sitting locked up inside the house, waiting for someone to knock before he will get up and answer. In God's house the door is always open so that those who even try to draw near will find more than a hint of hospitality and shelter. Recall that in Luke's parable of the prodigal son (Luke 15), the younger son, repentant of his sins and making his way back to his Father's house, doesn't even get to the porch. The Father sees him coming and rushes out to meet him!

Here is part of a traditional prayer of contrition, a prayer asking for forgiveness:

Celebrating the Sacrament

*O my God, I am heartily sorry for having offended you,
because I dread the loss of heaven and the pains of hell.
But most of all, because they offend you, my God,
who are all good and deserving of all my love....*

This traditional prayer speaks of two kinds of contrition. *Imperfect contrition* is when we are sorry for our sins primarily because we fear the *punishment* we deserve because of those sins. This imperfect contrition is expressed in the traditional act of contrition by the words, "My God, I am heartily sorry for having offended you, *because I dread the loss of heaven and the pains of hell.*" I sometimes describe imperfect contrition as the "child's reason" for being sorry. What I mean is that, ordinarily, your typical seven-year-old is sorry he has done something wrong because he has been caught and knows he will be punished. Obviously, this is neither the best nor the most mature form of contrition, but it is probably where most of us start.

Perfect contrition, the second kind of contrition, is expressed in the traditional prayer by the words, "My God, I am heartily sorry...*but most of all because [my sins] have offended you, my God, who are all good and deserving of all my love.*" Perfect contrition is the sorrow and regret we have for our sins because we know we have hurt someone. We feel the pain we have caused someone else, and the more we love that person, the more pain we feel. To contrast it with imperfect contrition, perfect contrition is sorrow of the "mature adult." A husband who has been angry with his wife may be sorry mostly because now she will be angry with him, give him the silent treatment, and otherwise ruin his day. This is imperfect contrition, and so it's clear that while someone may be an adult, they still have room to grow in the way they think of and treat others. Using this same circumstance, the more mature form of contrition—*perfect* contrition—is that felt by the husband who regrets his anger and lack of charity, not because he will suffer the painful consequences (a cold or overcooked supper?!), but because he knows that, through his attitude and action, *his wife* is suffering the consequences of *his* actions.

Again, what kind of contrition do we have? *Why* are we sorry for our sins? There may not be a clear answer to that question. The truth is that we adults live pretty complicated lives. We excel in some areas, we're noticeably poor in others, and we are probably "in the middle" with a lot of it all! That applies to our knowledge of ourselves, our relationships with others, and our confidence in and, yes, even our anxieties about, the mercy of God.

The good news is that God, through the Church, offers us reconciliation precisely because we don't "excel in all areas." After all, when we reach the legal age of adulthood, it doesn't mean we've learned it all. It means, hopefully, we have a somewhat better idea of the questions we need to ask about ourselves, others, and God. It means, hopefully, we have a desire to continue learning the skills that will make us truly mature adults. Maturing in our contrition is maturing in our relationship with God.

The sacrament of reconciliation is not meant for the perfect. "They" would have no need if it! When distinguishing between perfect and imperfect contrition, the Church is not so much engaged in a scholarly debate as it is trying to assure us that, if we can't be perfect (and we can't), then perfect contrition can always be our goal. The closer we come to it, the closer we come to loving God and loving our neighbor as ourselves.

Remember, the Church holds that even imperfect contrition is a grace from God, for it encourages and allows us to approach the sacrament and ask for and receive God's forgiveness. What a tremendous expression of God's generous love! The sacrament can supply what we lack. Paraphrasing a Jewish proverb, it's as though God is saying, "Come to me as far as you can, and I will meet you there."

Confession of Sins

The second essential part of the sacrament is acknowledging to the priest the sins of thought, word, act, or omission of which you are conscious. In the previous chapter, we briefly discussed "What do I need to confess?"[1] Before we consider this further, let's add something to our thoughts on contrition and on *why* we confess.

Put as simply as possible, we want to have an honest relationship with God. To use a powerful image from the opening pages of the Bible, we want to have that relationship with God that Adam and Eve had *before* they disobeyed God and ate that apple on the tree. What state were Adam and Eve in? Before their sin, they were before God, literally and figuratively, naked. The Bible tells us that this was neither the nakedness of shame nor of lust. It was, rather, the freedom of not having to conceal anything from God. They had nothing to hide! And what's the first thing Adam and Eve did after God found them out? They covered themselves, because now they did have something to be embarrassed about, something they thought they had to hide from God—and from each other. One way to look at our contrition, our coming to confession, is that it is our attempt, imperfect though it may be, to return to that relationship with God in which we need not be ashamed of his gaze nor be fearful of his response. God sees us as we are, yes, but his vision is better than ours, and so he also sees us as how we want to be. Wanting to cooperate with God's vision, a vision that does not keep us in the past but urges us on into a better future, is another way of understanding what we mean by contrition. We want to be "open" to God—open about our regret for the past and open about our hope for the future.

To return to *what* we have to confess. The Church teaches that we are not *required* to confess venial sins, but that doing so can be a great help as we try to live a better life. We *are* required to confess "each and every grave sin that [we] remember after an examination of conscience."

To actually "confess each and every grave sin" may not always be possible. Our memories are neither perfect nor precise, and we usually don't record our sins after we commit them. So what is the purpose and meaning of the requirement that we "confess each and every grave sin"?

What the Church is asking here is that we make an honest, "complete" confession—what canon law refers to as an "integral" confession. If we believe we have committed a mortal sin several times, we need to give the priest a reasonably accurate idea of how many times. Similarly, if we are conscious of having committed several different mortal sins, we do not have the option of choosing to confess only one and not mention the others. What we are striving for is honesty and integrity. A good confession (a canon lawyer would say a "valid" confession) requires that we are sorry for our sins, that we confess them, and that we intend to do our best to avoid them.

But the value of a complete or integral confession is not merely that it fulfills a requirement. An honest, integral confession gives the priest a better indication of your *life* (and not just your sins) and therefore helps him minister more directly, more effectively, to *you*. For example, if an unmarried man in his late twenties confesses that, since his last confession two years ago, he has had sexual relations, it is important for the priest to know whether the man is confessing an action he has committed once during the past two years, or three times, or many times. It is not a mathematical fact the priest is interested in but, rather, a clearer indication as to how much a part in this man's life this sin plays. It is not that one sin of impurity is alright (it isn't) or that ten or twenty times would be unforgivable (they can be forgiven). It is that, the better the priest understands the place these sins have had in the man's past, the better will he be able to advise him for the future.

Here is another example, one that emphasizes the value of the requirement while also clarifying what is not required. A penitent confesses she has not been to confession for a year, and that she has only been to Mass on Sunday a handful of times. She doesn't have to consult twelve months of calendars so she can say, "I missed Mass exactly 30 times." Her acknowledgment of attending Mass only a handful of times provides the priest with the information he needs, and that which the Church requires, for an honest and complete confession.

Act of Penance

The third essential part of the sacrament, the act of penance or satisfaction we are asked to make, reminds us that "absolution takes away sin, but it does not remedy all the disorders sin has caused" (*Catechism* 1459). Confession is about having our sins forgiven, but it is also about repairing, insofar as possible, the damage or hurt our sins have inflicted on others. The penance you accept and fulfill plays a part in this process of repair and restoration.

The act of penance "may suitably take the form of prayer, self-denial, and especially service to neighbor and works of mercy" (*Rite of Penance* 18).[2] Ideally, a penance "should serve not only as atonement for past sins but also as an aid to a new life and an antidote for weakness…[and it] should correspond to the seriousness and nature of [what has been confessed]" (18). Consequently, many priests will try to offer a penance associated in some way with the sins you have confessed. For example, if you have acknowledged you have treated a co-worker harshly, your penance might be to make a special effort to show him or her some act of kindness; in other words, to act toward them *now* as you should have acted toward them *then*. Likewise, if you confessed that last week you realized the grocery store clerk was undercharging you five dollars but you said nothing, the priest might suggest you either find a way to give the money back or, if that's not possible, put a few extra dollars in the basket during Sunday Mass or, perhaps, in the collection box many churches have for donations to the poor and needy. If you have admitted that you tend to be envious or jealous, you may be asked to think about the blessings you do enjoy and consider how you might share your gifts with those who have less. In each of these instances, the intention of the penance is two-fold: first, to encourage a new act of virtue rather than one of vice and, second, to try to "right a wrong." Whether your penance takes the form of a prayer or a specific act, it helps you put your faith into practice. We do confess with our lips, but true conversion comes from the heart. (In chapter 4, "Frequently Asked Questions," we will discuss what you might do if you think your penance is too difficult—or not difficult enough!)

THE CELEBRATION OF THE SACRAMENT OF PENANCE

We have considered three of the four essential parts of the sacrament, those three aspects that belong to you, the penitent. We now proceed step-by-step through the actual celebration of the sacrament, as it is outlined in the *Rite of Penance*.

1. Reception of the Penitent

The place where one goes to confession is traditionally called the *confessional* or, more recently, the *Reconciliation Chapel*. Depending on the structure of the church itself, this room is usually located near the entrance or along one or more of the side walls. The confessional or chapel allows you the choice of either talking with the priest face-to-face (sitting in a chair across from him) or, for those who may wish anonymity, behind a screen (and, usually, kneeling down).

When you enter, the priest may greet you with the words, "Peace be with you," or something similar. Some priests may say a short prayer or recite a verse from the Bible. Others, especially if you are confessing behind the screen, may simply wait for you to begin. Again, there is no one way to celebrate this sacrament, either for priest or penitent.

A simple way to begin is to make the Sign of the Cross and then say how long it has been since your last confession. If you're not sure or can't remember exactly when the last time was, give the priest the best idea you can.

2. Reading of the Word of God (Optional)

At this point, "the priest may read or say from memory a text of Scripture which proclaims God's mercy and calls [you] to conversion" (43). The text the priest recites may be only a few words ("Give thanks to the Lord for he is good and merciful."), or it may be a short passage from the Bible (a few verses from the parable of the prodigal son, for example). The *Rite of Penance* considers this an optional part of the celebration, and it is in fact many times omitted. (As mentioned above, some priests may greet you by reciting a text or verse.) Simply follow the priest's lead.

3. Confession of Sins and Acceptance of Satisfaction

Before you confess your sins, you may want to tell the priest something about yourself (if you have not already done so or if the priest doesn't know you). You don't need to tell him your name unless you want to, and this is especially true if you are confessing from behind the screen. The point here is simply to give your confessor some idea of what we call your "state in life" and "anything else that may help the confessor in the exercise of his ministry" (16). Here are some examples:

> *Father, it's been about two months since I last came to confession. I'm in my thirties, am married, and have two children. I'm mostly a homemaker, but I do some volunteer work here and there.*
>
> *It's been about six weeks. I'm a sophomore in college.*
>
> *I'm in my twenties, Father. My last confession? I guess it was Easter. I'm getting married soon, and my future wife and I wanted to start things off right.*
>
> *Father, I'm 35 years old. This is my second confession. My family and I entered the Church this past Easter.*
>
> *I'm upper-middle aged, Father. I'm married, and our last kid just went off to college.*

None of these introductions relates the penitent's life story, of course, but each one offers the priest some context into which he can place your confession.

You do not have to confess your sins in any particular order. For example, if you have examined your conscience according to the Ten Commandments, you do not need to start with the first commandment, proceed to the second, and so on. Some people prefer to confess first the sins that weigh most heavily upon them; others prefer to confess "from lesser to greater." Once again, the choice is yours. Here are two examples of how two gentlemen, each in their forties, each married with children, confess what are essentially the same sins, but each in his own style and in his own way:

> Peter: I *sinned against the third commandment ["You shall keep holy the Lord's Day"] once. I used the Lord's name in vain probably several times a week. I committed sins in thought against the ninth commandment ["You*

shall not covet your neighbor's wife"] a few times. I did tell a couple of lies, mostly harmless. I committed a venial sin against the fifth commandment ["You shall not kill"], when I drank a little too much at a party. For these and all the sins of my past life, I am truly sorry.

Paul: Father, the thing that bothers me the most is that I just don't always give my kids the kind of example I want to give them. My language isn't always the best. I know that they know I fudge a little on the truth, sometimes. Two things, in particular: I came home from a party last Saturday just a little bit woozy. Had a little too much to drink. Two of my kids saw that, I wish they hadn't. I made it even worse the next day, because I was really wiped out and just didn't bother to get up for Sunday Mass. Also, they don't know this of course, but I still have impure thoughts and desires at times. Most of all, I'd just like to be a better dad to my children. I think that is all, Father. I ask for your forgiveness.

Compare these two confessions and you will see that, for the most part, Peter and Paul confess the same sins. *How* they confess those sins is different, however, and so is the context in which they frame their confession. (Paul uses his responsibilities as a father as a key reference point with which to focus his confession.) Are both confessions good? Yes. Are both confessions "right"? Yes. So, what leads to these different ways of confessing? Several factors, probably most of all the particular kinds of religious formation or education each has had. The important thing is that both Peter and Paul came to the sacrament to seek forgiveness, and both confessed in an appropriate way. The point of the examples is not to assign a "higher grade" to one confession, but simply to illustrate the different ways in which sins can be confessed.

Here is another example of a penitent taking a moment to inform the priest about his "state in life" and "anything else that may help the confessor in the exercise of his ministry":

> Father, bless me. I think the last time I went to confession was about two years ago. I'm a sophomore in college and last week I made a retreat at the Newman Center. They talked a lot about how important it was for us to be thankful for our blessings. That really struck me. I guess I've got a better understanding now of how lucky I am to be here, and about the sacrifices my parents are making to send me here to college. Thinking about all of that, I realize—well, I wonder if my parents are really getting their money's worth. I waste a lot of time, and I know I could be a lot more serious about my studies—and my life, for that matter. The more I think about this, the more I want to do something more. Maybe it's time for me to grow up.

Our sophomore told his confessor some important things about himself, perhaps the most important being that he recently took part in a retreat that impressed him enough that he came back to confession after two years! Information such as this opens up wonderful possibilities for a discussion that can support and encourage his "wanting to grow up" in the Christian and spiritual sense. Once again, giving the priest information of this sort is not required. But it can be a better way to confess than simply reciting your sins: "better" because it can help the priest minister "better" to you.

After you have confessed your sins, the priest may ask you a question or two, or he may not. He may offer you specific advice about something you have mentioned, or simply give you a word or two of encouragement. Sometimes people are concerned about the questions the priest will ask. We'll consider this in some detail in the next chapter. For now, be assured that *if* the priest does ask

Celebrating the Sacrament

a question, it is because he believes he needs to know something more about what you have said in order to minister more effectively and more directly to you. And certainly you may ask the priest questions you have, either to better understand something he has said or to ask about something that concerns you.

Before asking you to make an act of contrition, the priest will give you a penance. We discussed this "act of satisfaction" earlier in this chapter, and will return to it briefly in the next.

4. Prayer of the Penitent and Absolution

The priest will ask you to make an act of contrition. In the confessional or Reconciliation Chapel of many parish churches, there is a card with one or more forms of an act of contrition that you may use. But you can use your own words, or any of the acts of contrition found in many prayer books. You need not proclaim a sermon! Your act of contrition may be as brief as, "Lord Jesus, Son of God, have mercy on me, a sinner." Or it may be longer, as the two examples below suggest.

> *O my God, I am heartily sorry, for having offended you, and I detest all my sins, because I dread the loss of heaven and the pains of hell. But most of all, because they offend you, my God, who are all good and deserving of all my love. I firmly resolve with the help of your grace, to confess my sins, to do penance, and to amend my life. Amen.*

> *My God, I am sorry for my sins with all my heart. In choosing to do wrong and failing to do good, I have sinned against you whom I should love above all things. I firmly intend, with your help, to do penance, to sin no more, and to avoid whatever leads me to sin. Our Savior Jesus Christ suffered and died for us. In his name, my God, have mercy.*
> (45)

The following are more examples of acts of contrition that, while brief, certainly express your regret for some of what you have done in the past and your desire to do better in the future.

Lord, you have given me so many gifts (skills, talents, friends, health, etc.), and I have not always been gracious in receiving those gifts or responsible in benefiting from them. I confess my sins, and ask for your grace in the days ahead.

Most loving God, as I ask you to forgive my sins, I ask also for the grace to love you, my family, my friends, and my neighbors with a sincere heart.

May I remember the mercy you have offered me, O God, and be willing to show that same forgiveness to those who have hurt me. And help me to remember that I can always try to be an instrument of peace to others rather than a cause of pain for them.

The priest will now say the formula of absolution. Fifty years ago, prior to the revision of the rite after the Second Vatican Council, the priest would say the words of absolution *at the same time* the penitent was making the act of contrition. Since the words of absolution are now in English, this small but significant change in the ritual allows you to hear these words of mercy and comfort:

God, the Father of mercies,
through the death and resurrection of his Son
has reconciled the world to himself
and sent the Holy Spirit among us
for the forgiveness of sins;
through the ministry of the Church

> *may God give you pardon and peace,*
> *and I absolve you from your sins*
> *in the name of the Father, and of the Son, +*
> *and of the Holy Spirit. (And you answer: Amen.)*

While the most important words the priest says are "I absolve you from your sins," it is helpful to consider the entire prayer of absolution. The words are few, but they convey some important truths. First, reconciliation is offered the penitent through God—a God who is not a cruel judge but, rather, a merciful Father. The prayer also reminds both penitent and priest that reconciliation is brought about through the supreme sacrifice offered by Jesus (his death) and, again, by the Father's loving power (Jesus' resurrection). The words of absolution stress the role the Holy Spirit plays in the forgiveness of sins and, by implication, the Spirit's continuing guidance in our lives. Finally, because the Church is a sign of God's presence on earth, reconciliation with him is asked for and given, not only through our individual hopes and private prayers, but through the public and official ministry of the Church.

5. Proclamation of Praise and Dismissal of the Penitent

The shortest and simplest part! After pronouncing the words of absolution, the priest will say words similar to what you hear at the end of Mass, for example, "Go in peace" or "God bless you." Your response? "Thanks be to God" or even a simple "Thank you, Father" are appropriate ways to conclude your confession.

The ritual ends here, but of course there is still something to be done: your "act of penance." On a historical note, it is interesting that, until about the tenth century, penitents would confess their sins, then go out and perform the penance assigned them (and this might take several days, weeks, or even months), and *then* come back to the church for the official act of reconciliation. Over time the process was simplified, the good intentions of the penitents were assumed, reconciliation was pronounced at the end of the confession, and the penitents were sent on their way to do their penance.

If the priest has given you some prayers as your act of penance, you may say those before you leave the church or, if you know that another time is better, at that time. And whether your act of penance consists of prayers that can be said right away or other actions to be performed later, it is recommended you spend a few moments in church thinking about what you have just done—and, especially, *about what God has done for you*. God has seen your sorrow, heard your desire to better your life, and forgiven your sins. Good reasons to linger in the church for a while and give God thanks!

Hopefully you now have a clear idea of how the celebration of the sacrament is carried out. As I have mentioned several times, "how to go to confession" should not be a source of anxiety. There is no one precise way of celebrating the sacrament, and you don't receive a poor grade if you "don't do the rite just right." The priest is there to help and guide you. He is, as the *Catechism* says, "not the master of God's forgiveness, but its servant" (1466).

I hope these first two chapters have addressed some of the concerns you may have had about the sacrament of reconciliation. I know from experience, however, that there are always more questions! We'll consider some of these in chapter 4.

Chapter Three

EXAMINATION OF CONSCIENCE

Just as there is no one precise way in which the sacrament must be celebrated, neither is there only one way to examine your conscience when preparing for it. Examinations of conscience are found in many prayer books and pamphlets and even on the Internet. The *Catechism* offers this insight regarding the examination:

> [Confession] ought to be prepared for by an *examination of conscience* made in the light of the Word of God. The passages best suited to this can be found in the Ten Commandments, the moral catechesis of the Gospels and the apostolic Letters, such as the Sermon on the Mount and the apostolic teachings. (*Catechism* 1454)[1]

WHAT IS AN EXAMINATION OF CONSCIENCE?

It is a consideration of how we are fulfilling our Christian obligations and responsibilities. It is a tool, an organized way to review, since our last confession, what we have done that we shouldn't have, and what we should have done that we haven't.

This examination is not meant to encourage scrupulosity or foster an obsessive guilt. Rather, it helps us continue to mature in the Christian life by calling us to a greater responsibility and accountability. When we examine our consciences, we are taking the time to take account of our lives.

Different Forms of an Examination of Conscience

One size doesn't fit all. Penitents approach the confessional from all directions and with different intentions. They come at different times and stages in their lives, and therefore come facing different issues, challenges, and situations. They come when their spiritual harvest is rich and when their spiritual resources seem to them meager.

Those who have been away from the sacrament for a long time may find an examination of conscience based on the Ten Commandments particularly helpful. Those celebrating the sacrament regularly, or those believing they are not great sinners but just lousy saints, may find more helpful an examination that asks them to consider the good works they have left undone (sins of omission). Others may find that an examination that refers to sinful attitudes in general rather than sinful actions in particular poses the more appropriate challenges to their growth now. Different formats help us discover new ways of thinking about where we are in relation to God and our neighbor.

Once you have decided *how* you will examine your conscience, the next question may be *when*? A daily examination of conscience (often before retiring for the night) has an established place in Catholic piety. When examining your conscience, specifically in preparing for confession, I suggest you do so twice: first, a day or two before you go to confession, and then again shortly before you actually enter the confessional or Reconciliation Chapel. This allows you some quiet time to consider what you want to say and how you want to say it. (For example, you may want to frame your confession around a particular aspect of your life, as we discussed in the previous chapter.)

In the following pages, I offer five models or formats of an examination of conscience. The fifth model focuses on what we consider "social sins," or how we are or are not contributing to the progress of society. This is an important consideration, for we must remember that we live, grow, and work in various communities (family, school, work, city, nation). And just as we are often pulled down by the weakness and sins of others (as others are undoubtedly weakened by us), sometimes we simply aren't aware of the good we can offer those communities. This final examination of conscience (one might also call it an "examination of opportunities") should not be seen as independent of any of the preceding four models. They can—and must—work together. Remember that the greatest commandment is "to love God *and* your neighbor." Remember also that, while we don't have to confess our less serious sins, acknowledging these ordinary, everyday offenses in the context of the sacrament can encourage and support our conversion and growth—and the good will in word and action we can offer to each other.

A. AN EXAMINATION OF CONSCIENCE FOCUSING ON GRAVE (MORTAL) SINS

People who have committed a mortal sin are not likely to forget it, but a structured examination of conscience can still be of some assistance, especially if it has been a long time since one's last confession. The following examination is based on a document published by the bishops of the United States in late 2006 titled *Happy Are Those Who Are Called to His Supper: On Preparing to Receive Christ Worthily in the Eucharist*. Arranged according to the order of the Ten Commandments, the document does not claim to provide an exhaustive list of mortal sins, but it does gives the more common examples of such. I have listed each of the commandments below. The examples from the bishops' document are printed in italics, and, in several cases, I have added an additional example or explanation. The complete document can be accessed from the bishops' Web site, which is listed in "Further Resources."

1. I am the Lord, your God, you shall not have strange gods before me.
    Believing in or honoring as divine anyone or anything other than the God of the Holy Scriptures.
2. You shall not take the name of the Lord, your God, in vain.
    Swearing a false oath while invoking God as a witness (e.g., perjury).
3. Keep holy the Lord's Day.
    Failing to worship God by missing Mass on Sundays and holy days of obligation without a serious reason, such as sickness or the absence of a priest. (Another example of a justifiable reason for missing Sunday Mass would be a parent staying home to care for a sick child or spouse.)
4. Honor your father and your mother.
    Acting in serious disobedience against proper authority; dishonoring one's parents by neglecting them in their need and infirmity.
5. You shall not kill.
    Committing murder, including abortion and euthanasia; harboring deliberate hatred of others; sexual abuse of another, especially of a minor or vulnerable adult; physical or verbal abuse of others that causes grave physical or psychological harm. (Producing, marketing, and using dangerous and illegal drugs would

also be considered serious sins against the fifth commandment.)
6. You shall not commit adultery.
   Engaging in sexual activity outside the bonds of a valid marriage.
7. You shall not steal.
   Stealing in a gravely injurious way, such as robbery, burglary, serious fraud, or other immoral business practices.
8. You shall not bear false witness against your neighbor.
   Speaking maliciously or slandering people in a way that seriously undermines their good name. (It is important to remember that telling "the awful truth" about someone without legitimate reason neither excuses nor justifies our comments. The accompanying footnote in the original source reproduces part of the *Catechism*'s discussion concerning "offenses against truth" as violations of the eighth commandment.)[2]
9. You shall not covet your neighbor's wife.
   Producing, marketing, or indulging in pornography.
10. You shall not covet your neighbor's goods.
    Engaging in envy that leads one to wish grave harm to someone else.

B. AN EXAMINATION OF CONSCIENCE FOR THOSE WHO BELIEVE THEY ARE "GOOD, BUT CAN BE BETTER"

As we have discussed, the sacrament of reconciliation is not only for those conscious of having committed grave sins. In fact, for most of us, our sins are of the ordinary, commonplace variety. Like the preceding examination, this one follows the order of the Ten Commandments, but the focus is on the opportunities we encounter—and the opportunities we pass up—to do something good.

1. I am the Lord, your God, you shall not have strange gods before me.

    What are my major preoccupations in life? Am I concerned about the right things? Do I take a few minutes each morning to thank God for the gift of a new day and consecrate that day to him? Simply: Do I make a conscious effort to include God in my day, every day?

2. You shall not take the name of the Lord, your God, in vain.

    How is my language? Do I use God's or Jesus' name in expressions of anger, or even as an expression of annoyance? If I stopped a moment before I spoke, might that extra moment help me express my feelings in a more respectful, more charitable way? If I am a parent, am I giving good example to my children by the way I speak?

3. Keep holy the Lord's Day.

    Every day is the Lord's, but is there anything special about how I spend my Sundays? Do I consider Sunday Mass enough to develop my relationship with God? Do I try to arrive at church a little early, to give myself time to settle down and prepare for Mass? Do I take a few minutes during the week to read and think about the coming Sunday's Gospel or about what *I* would say if I were preaching?

4. Honor your father and your mother.

    Whatever my age, do I pray for my parents? If I'm young, do I give them the benefit of the doubt when it comes to the instructions they give me? If I now have a family of my own, am I appropriately concerned about my parents' welfare? If one of my parents (or in-laws) has died, am I supporting their widow(er) insofar as I am able?

5. You shall not kill.

Am I caring for my health? Do I abuse alcohol, tobacco, or prescription medication? Do I make sure there is a designated driver when I've been "out for the evening"?

6. You shall not commit adultery.

How do I put my faithfulness to my spouse into practice? What evidence could my spouse present each day that I am helping our relationship grow?

7. You shall not steal.

Am I honest in my dealings with others? Do I correct any mistakes I have made in business, without waiting to see if I am "caught"? Do I respect the property of others? Am I willing to share what I have extra, especially with those who have not?

8. You shall not bear false witness against your neighbor.

How do I speak about others, particularly those whom I do not like—and may in fact have reason not to like? Do I enjoy hearing or passing on gossip? Do I keep confidences? Am I quick to judge when there is no need for me to judge?

9. You shall not covet your neighbor's wife.

Does the way I talk about others give my spouse reason to be jealous or otherwise concerned about our relationship? Do I respect proper boundaries in my relationships with my neighbors, associates, and co-workers? Do I linger over tempting thoughts or sexual images?

10. You shall not covet your neighbor's goods.

Am I grateful for what I have? Do I engage in useless, unhealthy competition with those around me?

Do I waste time and money just to acquire what others have? Do I congratulate others on their success and achievements?

C. AN EXAMINATION OF CONSCIENCE BASED ON THE "DEADLY SINS"— EVEN IF THEY HAVE NOT YET BECOME SO DEADLY IN YOUR LIFE

Christian tradition holds seven particular sins to be deadly or "capital" sins, so called "because they engender other sins, other vices"(*Catechism* 1866). The following examination focuses on our attitudes toward oneself and others as well as our actions.

- **Pride.** Do I compare myself with others in such a way that I put others down in my thoughts or words? Do I remember that my talents, skills, and abilities are gifts from God and something to be thankful for, rather than for self-exaltation? Do I thank others—through my words and actions—for the good they have done for me? What is my attitude toward those who are obviously less fortunate or less gifted than I am?
- **Avarice (or greed).** How do I use my extra resources? When I have enough of something, am I willing to make even a small sacrifice to help someone who might have less? Do I define myself by how much I have, or rather by how much I can give others? What are the things I want the most in life? Are these the right things?
- **Envy.** Do I resent the good fortune of others? Am I looking for ways to criticize those who have more (are more talented, more blessed, etc.) than I, so that I can "bring them down a notch"? Do the accomplishments of others make me jealous? Do I indulge in self-pity?

Examination of Conscience

- **Anger.** Do I control my temper? When I do have reason to be angry, do I express my anger in a way that is constructive and respectful? *For a parent*: Do I give my children a good example of what it means to be appropriately angry? When I am angry with my children, do I explain to them why I am angry with them? If my spouse and I quarrel in front of the children, do we take care also to "make up" in front of them?
- **Lust.** Do I feed the temptation toward lust by indulging in pornography or watching inappropriate movies or television shows? When I'm with my friends, how does my casual language about the opposite sex reflect how I see and consider them? Do I tell, or encourage the telling of, inappropriate jokes? How persistent am I in fighting the temptations of lust, whether they are temptations of thought or of actions with others or with oneself?
- **Gluttony.** Are my eyes regularly larger than my stomach, and so food is wasted? Do I drink to the point where I am not responsible for my actions? Does my drinking put myself or others in danger in any way? *For workers*: Does what I consume on my lunch hour allow me to continue with an honest day's work?
- **Sloth.** Am I satisfied with doing just enough to get by? Do I take advantage of the hard work of others to fill in what is lacking in my work? Do I put in an honest day's work? Is my boss (or my customer) getting their money's worth? Do I approach my various responsibilities (as a parent, employer, employee, and student) with appropriate care and seriousness?

D. AN EXAMINATION OF CONSCIENCE BASED ON SOME REFLECTIONS ON THE SCRIPTURES

This examination of conscience is based not only on specific actions as much as it is on our *attitudes* toward Jesus and ourselves. Ideally, you would select one or two passages listed below, read the entire account from your Bible, and then consider the questions posed. Because they focus on attitudes, these passages can be part of your review of your day at night, or as a way to wake up to the challenges and opportunities that await you as you begin a new day.

Matthew 5—7 has many verses that are helpful for examining one's conscience. Among them:

> *You are the salt of the earth....You are the light of the world.* Do I contribute to the common good? What kind of Christian example do I give those with whom I work? Am I honest in my dealings with others? Would my neighbors have enough evidence to "convict me of being a Christian"?
>
> *If you are bringing your offering to the altar and there remember that your brother has something against you, leave your offering there before the altar, go and be reconciled with your brother first, and then come back and present your offering.* These are among the most challenging words of Jesus in all the Gospels. We cannot separate love of neighbor from love of God. Remember what we pray: "Forgive us our trespasses *as we forgive* those who trespass against us."
>
> *Do not judge and you will not be judged....Why do you observe the splinter in your brother's eye and never notice the plank in your own?* Whenever we begin to evaluate

Examination of Conscience

others according to gospel standards, we are still missing the whole point of the Gospel!

Romans 12:14–21 charges us to treat others *better* than they treat us. Do I believe in this ideal? Do I try to put it into practice? Am I determined, as Saint Paul writes, "not to be conquered by evil but to conquer evil with good"?

Jeremiah 18:1–6 speaks of the potter who, when he encounters a lump of clay that is not formed just right, does not throw it away but continues to work it and shape it into the final form he wants. Jeremiah reminds his people that, as the potter does with his clay, so God does with us. *I thank God that he continues to work with me. What is my prayer to him? How do I want, how do I need, to be reshaped?*

Luke 5:1–11 is the account of the miraculous catch of fish, after which Peter pleads with Jesus to leave him, believing he is not worthy to be close to one who is so great. "Depart from me, O Lord," Peter says, "for I am a sinful man"—to which Jesus responds, "No." *I thank God for seeing beyond what I cannot do and urging me on to what, with his grace, I can do. I pray that, after I have confessed, I will allow Jesus to pick me up and lead me on according to his ways.*

Mark 10:46–52 presents the account of the blind beggar Bartimaeus. Some tried to keep him away from Jesus. Others said to him, "Take heart; rise, he is calling you." Jesus himself asked Bartimaeus, "What do you want me to do for you?" *I thank God for those who encourage and support me in my efforts. As I prepare for confession, how would I answer that question were Jesus to ask me, "What is it you want me to do for you?"*

Romans 8:31–39 asks the question, "Who can separate us from the love of God in Christ Jesus?" Saint Paul then goes on to list a whole series of things that *cannot* separate us from that love. *I thank God that he has promised he will have the last word* *in my life. But until that time, what are the things that get in the way between me and God?*

In **2 Corinthians 12:7–9**, Saint Paul writes about the "thorn in his flesh" that he has asked the Lord three times to take away. God didn't, and Saint Paul believed it was so that he would learn that God's grace and mercy is enough for him. *What is the "thorn in my flesh" that I can't seem to get rid of? How can I surrender more fully and confidently to that grace of God that can do all things?*

In **Mark 4:21–25** (also Matt 13:12 and Luke 8:16–18), Jesus remarks how foolish it is to light a lamp and then place it under a bed. *Humility would have us not call undue attention to ourselves, but do we allow the good we can do to remain undone because of timidity, a lack of confidence, or a lack of energy?*

There are several places in the Gospels where Jesus calms a storm or walks on water, but the account in **Matthew 14:22–33** may be especially significant for us. In this version Peter, too, begins to walk on the water. As he moves toward Jesus, however, his gaze turns from him to the dangers about him (the wind and the waves) and he begins to sink. *I ask for the gift of a faith that perseveres, and pray that throughout whatever storm I find myself in, my gaze remains fixed on Jesus.*

The account of Jesus healing the ten lepers in **Luke 17:11–19** reminds us not only of the power of God but also how easy it can be to turn into ourselves once we have received what we need. Only one leper returned to Jesus to offer him thanks. *I probably don't hesitate at all to pray when I need something. Am I as quick to express my thanks to God for the good things I have received? For the people in my life who sustain me?*

Matthew 18:23–35, the parable of the unmerciful servant, tells the tragic account of a servant whose huge debt was cancelled by his king simply because of the king's mercy. What wondrous generosity! But the servant apparently didn't realize forgiveness was a two-way street. We pray in the Lord's Prayer,

"Forgive us our trespasses as we forgive those who have trespassed against us." *Is this condition for our forgiveness reassuring to us, or is it a threat?*

The miracle of the loaves and the fish (the feeding of the multitude) is the only miracle found in all four Gospels. All accounts mention that the only food available was five barley loaves and two fish, but **John 6:1–15** adds the interesting detail that these meager supplies were brought by a little boy. At the end, the people had more than enough, as twelve baskets were needed to collect the leftovers. We focus on Jesus' power (which is certainly appropriate), but let's not forget that Jesus used what others—even a little boy—brought to him to do his work! *Do we trust, do we pray, that the Lord can take even the little we have to offer and, through his power, do great things?*

In **Matthew 13:24–30**, the parable of the weeds and the wheat growing together, Jesus warns against pulling up the weeds too early because doing so might pull up the wheat as well. We usually interpret the parable as referring to the final judgment at the end of all time when, in the words of another gospel passage, the sheep will be separated from the goats. But what happens if we apply this Gospel to ourselves now? *Just as we would not want someone to overlook the wheat in our lives because there are weeds in our field as well, how often do we focus only on the weeds in another's life, refusing to see, acknowledge, and appreciate the wheat that is there?*

The parable of the wise fool in **Luke 12:13–21** offers a haunting challenge to us all. We pray we will not die tonight (and most of the time our prayer will be granted!). But if tomorrow we were to receive the diagnosis of a disease that would kill us within six months or a year, how differently would we live the next six to twelve months? Would our values, our priorities, the way we spend our time, change? *Why wait until the diagnosis?*

E. AN EXAMINATION OF CONSCIENCE BASED ON MY RESPONSIBILITIES TO SOCIETY

We live in, depend on, and are influenced by various communities. This means that our relationship with these communities is a two-way street. Just as we benefit from their strengths and suffer from their weaknesses, so too are they better or lesser due to what we contribute and what we do not. It is one thing—a good thing, indeed—to be concerned about and charitable to those who live next door or down the block. It is another thing, equally good and essential for society, to concern ourselves about the "anonymous"—those who are "out there" and are needy, but with whom we have no personal relationship. I recommend the questions raised here be a regular part of an examination of conscience of all who have come "of legal age."

- **I have many things.** Do I think about how I can help those who do not? For example, the clothes I no longer want to wear, no longer fit, or need minor repairs: Do I simply discard them, or do I take the extra time and effort to put them in the hands of an agency that will distribute them to the needy? Another very simple, yet probably common example: Are there cans of food in my kitchen I probably will not use or that have been sitting there for months? As many have said, the "extras" simply taking up space in my house, basement, and garage are the things that those in need will not receive.
- **I am an employer or an employee.** Do I concern myself with the needs of my workers, and not just my legal obligations toward them? Do I promote an attitude and a practice of honesty and quality in what I sell to others? Certainly, I need to make a profit, but does my work truly profit others? Is my company or business able to

offer some charity to those (individuals or groups) that truly need it? Are these questions even being raised?

- **I am a citizen.** Do I take the time to educate myself in the substantive, rather than superficial, aspects of a political candidate's platform? Do I vote? Can I find the time to "bilaterally" support the election process, for example, by helping the elderly or the disabled make it to the polls? Do I express my perceptions about injustice in appropriate ways (e.g., conversation with and letters to public officials, appropriate participation in peaceful exhibitions)?
- **I live on this earth.** Do I do my part in complying with recycling programs? Do I needlessly overbuy or overuse? Do I teach my children or talk with my friends about "green" values and methods?
- **I live with others on this earth.** Do I allow the good I can contribute to be determined only by the legal standing of those who could benefit? Am I willing to decline, with an explanation, services from business corporations who discriminate because of race or creed?

I introduced this "social" examination of conscience by referring to our Lord's teaching that the great commandment is to love God *and* our neighbor. Perhaps an appropriate conclusion to this, and to all the forms of examination presented here, are the words of Saint Barnabas, as quoted in the *Catechism*:

> Do not live entirely isolated, having retreated into yourselves, as if you were already justified, but gather instead to seek the common good together. (1905)

Chapter Four

FREQUENTLY ASKED QUESTIONS

The previous chapters have presented a lot of information about the sacrament of reconciliation, but I'm sure all of your questions have not been answered. In this chapter, we'll address more questions people often ask about the sacrament, the confessor, and themselves as penitents.

Are there any sins that cannot be forgiven?

No. The New Testament is quite clear about this. Jesus did not come to condemn, but to forgive. We have the classic example of forgiveness within Jesus' inner circle itself. Although Peter denied Jesus three times, Jesus not only forgave him, he also made him "the rock" on which he built his Church.

It is true the Gospels do speak of an "unforgivable sin." In Saint Mark's Gospel, Jesus says that "people will be forgiven for their sins and whatever blasphemies they utter; but whoever blasphemes against the Holy Spirit can never have forgiveness, but is guilty of an eternal sin" (Mark 3:28–29; cf. Matt 12:31–32; Luke 12:10). The *Catechism* explains this by affirming that God's mercy has no limits, "but anyone who deliberately refuses to accept his mercy by repenting, rejects the forgiveness of his sins and the salvation offered by the Holy Spirit" (1864). This comment echoes a remark by Saint Augustine around the year 400: "He who created us without our help will not save us without our consent."

Has the priest really "heard it all"?

Most likely. Some people are sure their confession will shock or scandalize their priest but the truth is that, within a year or two after ordination, most priests will have heard just about every sin in the book. That includes the various sins of impurity, theft, physical assault, and even murder. Remember that the priest does not expect people to come to confession to tell him how good they are! And, of course, the important thing is not that your priest has probably "heard it all," but that he is able to absolve you of these sins.

What if I think my confession is going to take a long time or want it to take some time?

If you are concerned about this, then it is an indication that you don't want to just rush in and rush out but are taking your confession seriously. You are also taking into consideration those who may be inconvenienced by what you anticipate may be a longer-than-usual confession.

If this is your situation, you might begin your confession by telling the priest, "Father, I think this may take a little time, and I want you to know there are other people waiting to come in." This helps your confessor decide how he might best proceed and help you at this time.

Another possibility would be to wait until all others have confessed. Of course, if you enter the confessional fifteen minutes before the Saturday evening Mass, your confessor will be between that rock and a hard place. He'll certainly want to minister effectively to you, but he'll also need to respect the parishioners waiting for the scheduled Mass.

If you think your confession is going to take longer than usual—perhaps it has been a long time since you have been to confession, or you have a complicated matter you would like to put before the priest—then your best approach might be to call the rectory and set up an appointment. This way you can take your time, and neither you nor the priest will feel rushed by the ticking clock or others waiting in line. The priest may suggest you meet in his office, but if you would still prefer to confess behind the screen, tell the priest that. Confessing behind the screen is an option that should always be available to you.

How long should a confession take?

As long as it needs to! Each confession—and each penitent—is unique. Some confessions, especially those of people who approach the sacrament with some regularity, may be simple and uncomplicated. A "simple" confession does not mean it is not an important confession. Such a confession might require only a few minutes to be celebrated with the appropriate care and reverence. On the other hand, if you have questions or are looking for advice on a particular situation—or, again, if it has been a long time since you've been to confession and you feel you have a lot to say—the confession is obviously going to take longer. Long or short, the significance of a confession is not determined by its length. After all, the effectiveness of a visit to your physician is not measured by how long the appointment is. "How long should a confession last?" my students ask. As long as it needs to.

How often should I go to confession?

If you do not believe you have sinned gravely (mortal sin), how often you come to confession will depend in large part on what the sacrament means to you and, perhaps, what grace or particular assistance you are looking for. Remember, the sacrament of reconciliation needn't be understood primarily as "emergency surgery." For many Catholics, it is a spiritual and prayerful exercise regularly available to us so that we can manage our spiritual health and growth.

If you are returning to the sacrament after a long time, you might find it helpful to reestablish a habit of confessing once a month or so. Again, others who are not conscious of having committed grave sins may find the beginning of the seasons of the year or the liturgical seasons of Advent, Lent, and the return to

Ordinary Time during the summer a helpful standard. Still others—for example, those experiencing a particularly difficult time in their lives—may find monthly or even more frequent confession a help.

Should I confess face-to-face or behind the screen?

What works better for you? Confessing face-to-face ordinarily suggests to the priest that you are open to some discussion about what you have confessed. The face-to-face approach encourages such conversation and often makes it easier. On the other hand, the anonymity that confessing behind the screen offers is reassuring for some people. It certainly does not automatically rule out the possibility of a dialogue between you and the priest.

Interestingly, some people prefer to confess behind the screen for reasons other than anonymity. I've been told by several parishioners that confessing while kneeling behind the screen seems more appropriately penitential to them, or that it allows them to focus more on their confession to God by helping them concentrate more on what they want to say rather than worrying about the priest's reaction.

Face-to-face or behind the screen? Which option encourages you to approach the sacrament? The most important thing is that you celebrate the sacrament as you are able to do so.

What must I confess? What can I confess?

We discussed these two questions at some length in the first chapter. To summarize:

> All mortal sins of which penitents after a diligent self-examination are conscious must be recounted by them in confession, even if they are most secret and have been committed against the last two precepts of the Decalogue ("You shall not covet your neighbor's wife, nor his goods").

> [A]fter having attained the age of discretion [the age at which it is judged a young child has enough knowledge and experience to distinguish right from wrong, traditionally regarded as around seven years of age], each of the faithful is bound by an obligation faithfully to confess serious sins at least once a year.
>
> Without being strictly necessary, confession of everyday faults (venial sins) is nevertheless strongly recommended by the Church. Indeed the regular confession of our venial sins helps us form our conscience, fight against evil tendencies, let ourselves be healed by Christ and progress in the life of the Spirit. By receiving more frequently through this sacrament the gift of the Father's mercy, we are spurred to be merciful as he is merciful. (*Catechism* 1456–58)

What about the sins of my past life I've already confessed? Especially serious, or mortal, sins?

Once you have confessed a sin and have received absolution, the sin is forgiven. No matter how serious the sin may have been, there is no *obligation* for you to confess it again. But while the Church does not require that a sin once forgiven be confessed again, there are times when you might feel a need to do so.

In the past, many Catholics were taught to conclude their confession with a formula such as, "For these and all the sins of my past life, especially for the sin of…, I am truly sorry." This readmission of past sins is not required, but it is an acceptable practice. And for some, it reflects their advancing in wisdom as well as their growing in years. For there are sins we have confessed and for which we have been sacramentally forgiven that, nevertheless, continue to occupy a not-so-peaceful place in our minds and hearts.

For example, young adults now facing parental responsibilities themselves often come to appreciate more the sacrifices their parents made, as they also realize how they could have better honored them. (Maybe this awareness is an example of what we mean by "growing pains"!) Older adults may find themselves caring for a parent notably weakened in body or mind, an experience that can challenge them to remember and return the loving care given them decades previously.

"For these and all the sins of my past life, especially for…." Such an admission does not deny the divine forgiveness already granted a confessed sin. Nor does it reflect a nagging guilt that just won't go away. Our sins are forgiven through the sacrament, but often our regret for the hurt those sins have caused is not something we can, nor wish to, entirely dismiss. Our memories of sins confessed need not chain us to the past, but can contribute to those growing pains that urge us on to live and act now as we wish we would have years ago. These memories remind us of those "second and third chances" that are always part of our never-ending conversion.

What if the priest asks me an embarrassing question?

Priests try to be careful when asking questions in the confessional. If and when a priest asks a question, it is not because he is merely curious or is trying to pry needlessly into personal details. A priest may ask a question because something you have said isn't quite clear to him. He may ask a question because he believes he needs to know something more about what you are confessing. Remember that the priest is concerned not just about your sin, but about *you*.

For example, if you confessed, "I really lose my temper with my family a lot," the priest might ask you to explain a bit more what you mean. What is he looking for? He may simply want to get a better idea of what you mean by "losing your temper." Getting frustrated is one thing. Shouting for ten minutes is another. Becoming combative is something else again. So the priest may ask a question, not out of idle curiosity, but because he wants to understand better what you are confessing. The better he understands where you are coming from, the better he can direct whatever advice or encouragement he offers to you and not to an abstract, generic sin of anger.

Priests will ask questions in the confessional because they believe you are taking your confession seriously and they want to take you seriously. I remember talking with a group of college-age women about their experience in going to confession. "What's the most important thing that priests should remember when they're hearing your confession?" I asked them. "Tell priests it's not easy for us to say our sins," they all agreed. I then asked if that meant they'd prefer the priest not make any comments or ask any questions at all—just "listen and absolve." One of the young women said it well: "He shouldn't *keep* asking. But, you know, sometimes we wish he would ask a question or two. I mean, it's difficult for us to say what we want to say and, well, sometimes we need some help." One of her friends added this comment:

> What's really disappointing is when you've mustered up the courage to go ahead and say something and you actually want to talk about it—at least a little—and the priest just lets it hang. When it's something I was afraid of, but really wanted to talk about, I don't leave the sacrament relieved. I leave feeling I've wasted my time. Wasn't he interested—really interested—in what I was saying? Did he think I was just doing this as a matter of routine?

Many times a priest will ask you a question to see if you want to say something more about what you have confessed. Any professional in a counseling situation knows that many times people want to talk about a specific point, but aren't quite sure how to bring it up, and hope their counselor or director can pick up their hesitation and their willingness and help them through.

But what should you do, what can you do, if the priest asks you something you truly believe is "none of his business," or a question you find very difficult or terribly embarrassing to answer? In that case, it's appropriate to say something like, "Father, that's a really embarrassing question" or, "Father, that's really personal, it's hard to answer" or even a respectful, "Father, I'd rather not talk about that if I don't have to." Most priests will understand immediately what you are saying (and feeling) and move away from the matter with an apology. If the priest persists, however, and you remain convinced that his question is inappropriate, the situation is unfortunate. I would like to believe these situations are extremely rare. And I know there are other confessors available.

The key points to remember are: (1) the priest asks a question because he wants to minister more effectively to you; (2) priests understand that many people find going to confession difficult; (3) a "bad" question is likely a "thoughtless" question, not a deliberate, ill-intentioned one; and (4) it is *your* confession and the priest's responsibility is to minister to you on behalf of the Church in the name of Christ. So help him to help you. If you have trouble answering a question for whatever reason, let him know. He will know what to do.

What if the priest refuses to give me absolution?

Some people fear the priest will not give them absolution because they continue to commit the same sins time and again. Others may hesitate to approach the sacrament because they do not want to be dishonest: they are sorry for the sins they have committed but are doubtful they will really be able to avoid those sins in the future. They don't want to make a "bad confession" by making a promise they won't be able to keep, and so they don't go.

The fear is understandable. But let's remember that we have a sacrament of reconciliation because we need it. The sacrament is for us: sinners, imperfect people, men and women who try and fail—and want to try again. When we go to confession, we're not claiming success. We're proclaiming our intention to do better and acknowledging that we need God's grace to help us. No priest expects a penitent to leave the confessional and live a perfect life. No priest will ask a penitent for any such guarantee. God does not ask us to do the impossible, and neither will the priest. In fact, a Vatican document written specifically to assist priests in their ministry in the confessional states what priests know well: that they are to "avoid demonstrating lack of trust either in the grace of God or in the dispositions of the penitent, by exacting humanly impossible absolute guarantees of an irreproachable future conduct" (*"Vademecum* for Confessors 3,11).[1]

In other words, when you go to confession, you are not promising you will live a perfect life in the future. You are acknowledging you have sinned and that you will do what you can, as best as you can, to live more according to God's law. The priest will take your coming to confession itself as one indication that you are sorry for your past sins and want to do better.

What if my penance seems too harsh or if it doesn't seem to be enough?

It can be difficult for a priest to offer you a penance that is "just right." Priests don't consider the penance as punishment but, as we noted in an earlier chapter, a "remedy for sin and a help to renewal of life."

If you think your penance is too much—that is, it would take too much time to perform, or is too difficult, or you simply don't have the resources to carry out the penance—you should tell that to the priest. He may ask you why you think it is too much, but he will likely adapt the penance to your circumstances or suggest a new penance altogether.

Similarly, feel free to tell the priest if you think you should be doing something more than the penance he suggests. This doesn't happen often, but it could well invite an interesting discussion about what God does for us in the sacrament and what our response might be. And of course, whether or not you mention this to the priest, you are always permitted to do more than the penance assigned!

What if I forget my penance? Or, after my confession, I realize that the priest didn't give me a penance?

Maybe you were preoccupied when the priest gave you a penance (perhaps you were trying to remember if you had confessed everything) or, similarly, the priest neglected to give you a penance because he was momentarily distracted. In either case, spending a few moments in church afterward allows you the opportunity to say a traditional, time-honored penance such as an Our Father, Hail Mary, and Glory Be to the Father, or perhaps a decade of the rosary. You might also want to think again about your confession, and identify the sin for which you are most sorry or that is the most serious. For example, if the sin you regret the most is that you spoke harshly about someone, you might say a prayer for that person—and promise yourself that you will find something good to say to him or about him in the next day or two.

What if I forget to confess something serious?

Forgetting to confess something is not a sin. Should that happen, simply mention it the next time you celebrate the sacrament. In the meantime, there is no reason to worry or feel anxious. We need the sacrament because we are not perfect, and so it shouldn't surprise us that sometimes we confess imperfectly. (And again, remember that it is not necessary to confess each and every venial sin. Only mortal sins *must* be confessed.)

My memory isn't what it used to be. Should I write down my sins so that I remember them all?

If you find writing down your sins helps you make a good confession, you may do so. Of course, be sure that you destroy the list after your confession. God doesn't keep track of your sins once you have confessed, and there's no reason for you to keep a record of them either. Once again, if you honestly forget to confess a serious sin, you can confess it the next time you go to confession. Forgetfulness is annoying, but in itself it isn't sinful.

It's been a long time…and I don't know what to do. I don't know where to start.

That may be all you need to say as you begin your confession. The priest is there to help you, not grade you on your sacramental performance. For the priest, one of the most important things about your coming to confession is that *you are there!* Don't hesitate to ask him for help.

I need to confess something that is really embarrassing, something that's really hard to put into words. What should I do?

One thing you might do is tell the priest exactly that. He is there to *minister* to you, and he wants you to make a good confession as much as you want to.

Sins against purity are not easy to talk about. The priest knows this, and if you tell him you're having trouble confessing something in this regard, you may be sure he will take extra care in hearing your confession. You might consider giving him a "clue," something along the lines of, "Father, I have something that's really difficult to talk about, it involves the sixth commandment" (that is, "You shall not commit adultery," which traditionally refers to various sins of impurity).

Finally—and this will likely come as a surprise to many penitents—what stands out in *your* mind when you make your confession may be your guilt or embarrassment. *What makes the biggest impression on the priest, however, is your humility and your courage in confessing.*

What if I don't know if I've committed a sin or not?

Traditional moral theology tells us that if we are not sure we have committed a mortal sin, we ordinarily enjoy the benefit of the doubt and can reasonably assume we have not. Again, a mortal sin is a deliberate, willful act, not something we "back into." If this answer isn't too satisfying, you can always bring it up and talk with your priest about it.

But I commit the same sins over and over again.

Of course. Most of us do! Confession usually won't give us *the* answer to the problems we have or show us *the* remedy for the sins we confess. We may recite the same sins from one confession to the next, but that doesn't mean the sacrament has failed us. Reconciliation offers us the assurance of divine forgiveness, not the guarantee of human perfection.

Think about it this way. If you know you often do something that annoys your spouse or your best friend, you know also how important it is for you to apologize again…and again. Imagine their reaction if one day you said, "Hey, I know this particular thing I do really annoys you. I'm tired of saying that I'm sorry. So, from now on, when I do it, just remember that I am sorry, even if I don't say it." Such an attitude doesn't really do much for your spouse or friend—or, ultimately, for you.

Committing old sins again doesn't mean we've lost the battle. Saint Paul, frustrated that the thorn in his flesh still remained even after he had three times asked the Lord to take it away, realized all the more how dependent he was on God's grace and mercy (2 Cor 12:7–9). Sometimes our frequent sins can be frequent reminders to us of our need to be humble—and to forgive those who have sinned against us.

What about communal penance services?

The technical title of a communal penance service is, "Rite for Reconciliation of Several Penitents with Individual Confession and Absolution." Many parishes offer these celebrations during Advent and Lent. The *Rite of Penance* explains that this way of celebrating the sacrament shows more clearly the ecclesial nature of penance:

> The faithful listen together to the word of God, which
> as it proclaims his mercy invites them to conversion;
> at the same time they examine the conformity of their

lives with that word of God and help each other through common prayer. (22)

A communal celebration of reconciliation ordinarily begins with a hymn and a prayer, and includes a reading (or readings) from the Bible, a homily, and very often a general examination of conscience led by the priest or another minister. Those who choose then make their private confession to the priest, receiving from him their penance and sacramental absolution.

At a communal celebration of the sacrament of penance, you remain obligated to confess "each and every mortal sin" of which you are aware. As always, if you are not conscious of having committed any mortal sins, you are free to choose which venial sins you will confess. (And remember that venial sins—those ordinary, everyday sins—are forgiven also by prayer, participating in the Eucharist, and works of charity.)

Because there are usually many people attending a communal celebration of reconciliation, it is not the best time to confess if you wish to discuss your confession with the priest in any detail, or if you are asking for advice about a complicated situation.

Is a communal penance service the same as general absolution?

No. As indicated previously, while there are communal aspects to a penance service, parishioners seeking sacramental absolution approach a priest individually to confess their sins, receive their penance, and have the words of absolution pronounced over them.

General absolution, known technically as "Rite for Reconciliation of Penitents with General Confession and Absolution," involves no individual confession of sins. Instead, those present make a general act of contrition and confession (such as the "I confess" we sometimes pray at the beginning of Mass), after which the priest pronounces absolution over all present.

The Vatican has strictly limited the occasions on which general absolution is permitted. In the United States, the most likely scenario is when the danger of death is imminent and there is not enough time for those wishing to confess to do so individually. I say "most likely" because, fortunately, in our country such situations are few and far between.[2] A second situation in which general absolution is permitted is when, if general absolution were not given, "the faithful would be forced to be for a long time without the grace of the sacrament or without communion" (*Rite of Penance* 31b).

This statement can be confusing. The key phrase is "for a long time." For example, you attend a communal penance service in your parish on Tuesday and many more people than expected are at the service. Or you are on a pilgrimage with a large group from your parish and there is the unexpected opportunity to attend Mass at the site of a most sacred shrine. Due to circumstances, however, the priest must begin Mass within 15 minutes and there is insufficient time for the large number of people who want to confess. May general absolution be given in either of these two situations? The Church's *Code of Canon Law* says no. The rationale is that while people cannot confess individually *at that time*, they presumably would have the opportunity to do so before *a long time* has gone by.[3]

One aspect of general absolution some people do not always understand is that it is a *temporary concession*, a *pastoral allowance*, in the face of a specific situation. The Church does not understand it, nor does she present it, as a regular alternative to the individual confession and absolution essential in a communal penance service (or, naturally, in an individual confession). In line with this, for a general absolution to be valid, the parishioner must intend to confess individually his or her grave sins at the next possible opportunity. (Remember that venial sins can be forgiven by various means, including general absolution.)

The *Code of Canon Law* has three canons that lay out the

requirements for the celebration of general absolution. Readers interested in this will likely not have ready access to the *Code of Canon Law*, and so I have included the canons in this footnote.[4]

Should I go to communion if I've committed a mortal sin and haven't had a chance to go to confession?

Two entries in the Church's *Code of Canon Law* help us answer this question. The first canon states that sacramental confession is necessary prior to receiving the Eucharist unless "there is a grave reason" to receive communion and "there is no opportunity to confess" (916).[5] The second canon states that confession and absolution "constitute the only ordinary means by which a member of the faithful conscious of grave sin is reconciled with God and the Church," and that only "physical or moral impossibility" excuses us from this, in which case "reconciliation can be obtained by other means" (960).[6] Let's consider these important canons point by point.

First, Church teaching holds that grave sins ordinarily are forgiven only by confession to a priest and the sacramental absolution given by him.

Second, if there is a *grave reason* for going to communion *and* there is no opportunity to confess, a person may receive communion if they make an act of perfect contrition, with the intention of confessing to a priest at the next opportune time.

Third, the canons allow communion to be received under these circumstances and with this intention. They do not require that one receive communion; they allow it for a grave reason. This allowance is not a substitute for individual confession and absolution. It is, rather, a temporary concession, given because of human weakness and a particular circumstance.

How might these canons be applied in a concrete situation? Let's consider an example of the concession the canon allows in the case of a "physical impossibility." A woman, suffering a heart attack, is in intensive care. Her condition is critical. A priest has not been able to see her yet, but one of the parish's eucharistic ministers comes to visit and offer her communion. May she receive? Yes. She feels a grave reason to receive our Lord in the Eucharist: she is frightened, afraid she may die. She cannot confess to the extraordinary minister (though she can pray with him or her), and she cannot go to church to go to confession (a "physical impossibility"). In this situation, she may say an act of perfect contrition and receive communion, with the intention of confessing her sin to a priest as soon as is practicable.

Let's consider a second example, that of a "moral impossibility." The father of a priest is in intensive care. Like the woman in the preceding example, he is frightened that death may be near. The priest—his son—arrives at the hospital with communion. The father knows he is guilty of the sin of adultery, but he cannot imagine confessing this grave offense against his wife to their son. May he receive? Yes. The man's relationship with the available confessor—his son—makes it extremely difficult, if not psychologically impossible, for him to confess his sin (a moral impossibility). He, too, may say an act of perfect contrition and receive communion, with the intention of confessing to (another) priest as soon as one is available.

Let's consider a case where it's not quite a "life or death" matter. Parents are going to Sunday Eucharist with their four children, their youngest of whom is to make his first communion with his classmates at the Mass. One parent, conscious of having sinned gravely, plans to go to confession at the scheduled time, shortly before Mass begins. As things turn out, however, more people than usual have the same idea and time runs out. The priest leaves the confessional and begins to vest for Mass. May the parent receive the Eucharist? Yes. The parent has a grave—not a life or death, but a serious, an important—reason for wanting to go to communion with the family on this most special day. The parent is not trying to avoid confession, but there is simply neither the time nor the opportunity to confess (again, a physical impossibility). After making an act of perfect contrition and resolving to confess at the next opportunity, the parent may in good faith receive the Eucharist.

These examples illustrate what the two canons mean. To summarize: if there is a "grave reason" for receiving communion and there is a "grave reason" why one cannot first go to confession (physical or moral impossibility), an act of perfect contrition, accompanied by the resolution to confess as soon as possible, allows one to receive. Again, these conditions are a pastoral concession to receive the Eucharist, not an alternative to sacramental confession.

Will the priest really keep secret what I have told him?

Absolutely. Preserving the "seal of confession" is among the most sacred obligations a priest has, and the absolute secrecy of the confessional is drilled into seminarians from the beginning of their training. In the classroom, I often ask the question, "What are the exceptions to the seal of confession?" simply to emphasize that *there are no exceptions*.

The priest's situation is unique here when compared to other professions such as psychiatrists and counselors. These men and women also have a privileged relationship with their clients but, according to the law, they must inform the proper authorities or take action under certain circumstances, for example, if their client admits physically or sexually abusing a minor. *Under the seal of confession, however, there are no exceptions.* Whatever sins a penitent confesses to a priest in the sacrament remains under the seal, and this applies even after the death of the penitent. So strict is the Church in this regard that a priest who intentionally and directly violates the seal of the confession is automatically excommunicated.

Let's continue to discuss the protection the seal of confession offers penitents. A priest cannot speak to a penitent outside of the sacrament and refer to, or ask about, something the penitent has previously confessed. For example, Judy comes to me for confession on Saturday afternoon and confesses she stole a few dollars from her cash register. As a penance, I ask her to return the money. A week later, I see Judy after Sunday Mass. I cannot ask her, "Have you returned that money yet?" To do so would be to take sins confessed and "move them outside" the confessional—in other words, break the sacramental seal.

Here is another example to emphasize the privacy the seal of confession guarantees the penitent. In his confession, John tells me he has been drinking heavily and wants help. I suggest, among other things, that John consider attending an AA meeting or two. Later on I happen to remember that there's a particularly good pamphlet dealing with this problem in the rack in the church vestibule. (Now why didn't I think of that during John's confession?!) So, may I tell John about it the next time I see him? Again, the answer is clearly no. *If* John comes to me and he says something like, "My confession the other day, thanks, do you have any other suggestions?" (and if I do, in fact, remember his confession), then I can recommend the pamphlet. By mentioning it, he "opens the door" of the confessional to the two of us, so to speak. But *I* cannot open that door outside of confession. It must be at his initiative.

The following example, a classic one, is even more illustrative:

> A confessor knows that a certain person is a compulsive thief. The confessor is later appointed the pastor of a parish where that person is on the parish finance council. The pastor may not remove the person based on knowledge gained solely from the confession.[7]

To summarize: the priest is solemnly bound to keep secret whatever sins you have confessed in the confessional—even after your death.

By the way, should you become aware of what someone else has confessed—for example, through accidentally overhearing the confession—you are obliged to maintain the secrecy of the confessional. This obligation is quite understandable, as it is the courtesy and respect for privacy you would want from others if the situation were reversed.

But does the priest really forget what I've confessed?

Many times, it is as simple as that. An hour, a half-hour, ten minutes after your confession, the priest really has no "active memory" of your confession. I know it's difficult for people to understand how this works. I've been ordained more than thirty years, and I still can't give an explanation that satisfies me! Perhaps an analogy will help.

Your neighbor a few houses down is also your physician. A few days after you've had your annual physical under her care, the two of you are enjoying the hospitality at another neighbor's party. Is your physician-neighbor preoccupied with your physical examination? No. Why not? The *context* is different. And in this different context, your physician does not see you as a body she has examined or a set of lab results she has reviewed. She sees you as a person, a neighbor, a friend—just as you see her as a neighbor and friend. Similarly, if you changed the context—let's say you pull her aside and say, "I want to discuss that pain I was telling you about"—then the chances are good that your physician will be able to enter immediately into a discussion with you about that. You have brought back a different context to your conversation. It works much the same way when it comes to confession. In the seminary community in which I teach, I often assist at reconciliation services. Shortly thereafter I may encounter in the halls someone whose confession I have heard. Do I think of what he told me? No. The context is different. In my experience, this is the way it is almost all the time.

Obviously, there are confessions that the mind cannot easily set aside. To completely and immediately forget that one is hearing someone confess to abusing a child would require an exercise of mind and will of which few are capable. Nevertheless, even though I may not absolutely and immediately forget this confession, I remain bound by the seal of confession. And, as I addressed in an earlier chapter, the penitent's sin is not necessarily what makes the lasting impression on me.

Aren't there some sins that are "reserved"?

The *Baltimore Catechism*, a textbook familiar to older generations of Catholics, noted that while a priest has the power to forgive all sins confessed, "he may not have the *authority* to forgive all [sins]" (emphasis mine). To forgive sins validly in confession, the *Catechism* explains, a priest needs both the power and the authority to use the power:

> The sins which the priest has no authority to absolve are called reserved sins. Absolution from these sins can be obtained only from the bishop, and sometimes only from the Pope, or by his special permission. Persons having a reserved sin to confess cannot be absolved from any of their sins till the priest receives faculties or authority to absolve the reserved sin also.[8]

When the Church revised the *Code of Canon Law* in 1983, the use of the term *reserved sin* was discontinued. The concept underlying it, however, remains. Basically, it holds that some offenses are so serious that, while they can be forgiven, a censure or penalty is attached to them that must be removed by an appeal to a higher authority than the parish priest—that is, the diocesan bishop or, in some cases, the Holy See. (Hence, the former term, that the sin was "reserved" to the bishop or to Rome.) I'm probably providing more information here than you will ever need to know! However, in answer to the question…

There are five sins that incur a penalty or censure, the removal of which is reserved to the Holy See. These sins are the desecration of the Blessed Sacrament, physical violence against the pope, a priest absolving a sexual partner, a priest directly violating the seal of confession, and a bishop unlawfully consecrat-

Frequently Asked Questions

ing a bishop. These are extreme cases and, obviously, the last three can be committed only by priests or bishops.

Four additional sins are considered serious enough that, depending on the circumstances, they carry the penalty of excommunication. These are the sins of apostasy, heresy, schism, and the procurement of an abortion.[9] Of these, the procurement of an abortion is one that priests and penitents will most likely encounter in the confessional today.

The gravity attached to this sin will hopefully not discourage you from approaching the confessional and your priest. The pain that can linger for years following an abortion is all the more reason to seek the forgiveness that the sacrament expresses and effects, and to take advantage of the healing it offers. To again appeal to a medical analogy: abortion is certainly a serious wound suffered by all involved in the decision and the act, and the healing of this wound takes time and is itself painful. The Church tries to ease the path to sacramental forgiveness and spiritual healing with a pastoral concession. In many (if not most) dioceses in the United States, your parish priest has both the power (from his ordination) to forgive the sin as well as the faculty or authority (from his bishop) to remit the attached penalty. In other words, the priest may absolve the sin and remove the excommunication (if one was incurred) during the course of a confession.[10] The following statement is typical of the sacramental policy in many U.S. dioceses: "The faculty [authority] is given to remit in the internal forum [in sacramental confession] and within the Diocese the following automatic penalties…the excommunication of a person who procures a successful abortion."

As we conclude this section on "Frequently Asked Questions," it is appropriate to refer to the very first question and answer and note that there is no sin, no matter how serious or offensive it may be, that cannot be forgiven. Jesus did not come to condemn, but to heal.

Epilogue

HEARING CONFESSION

I remember my grade school religion teachers reassuring my classmates and me that we should be neither afraid nor ashamed to confess our sins. "Father has heard them all, children, you won't scandalize him!" Occasionally, our parish priests would offer encouragement from their unique perspective, describing time spent in the confessional as a sure cure for insomnia. It seemed that even the youngest priests claimed that hearing confessions was "the most boring job in the world."

I have no doubt these teachers and priests had the best of intentions. They wanted us to make a good confession and were trying to soothe our young souls as we got ready to march over to the church for an encounter we did not exactly look forward to. I hope our words of reassurance these days are more optimistic! And that is precisely my intention here. Many of us know what going to confession is like. But what is it like to *hear* confessions? What is it really like from "the other side of the screen"?

NO SCANDAL, NO BOREDOM

I've been ordained over thirty years, more than enough time to have heard countless confessions of grave offenses against God, self, neighbor, and enemy. I guess I have "heard it all." And my teachers those many years ago were right: I have not been scandalized, but neither have I been bored. On the contrary, I have been impressed.

What impresses me as I sit in the confessor's chair is not what I hear people telling me they have done (their sins), but rather what I see happening: the grace of God at work!

Certainly, I have been told things that certainly were difficult and embarrassing for my penitents to admit. What amazes me, however, is the courage and honesty with which they confront their sin.

I have listened to lengthy, detailed admissions of laxity, irresponsibility, lack of charity, and malice. What I remember, though, is the humility that leads one to make such a thorough examination of conscience and resolve to do better.

I have found myself absolving people whom I knew to be holier than I. It takes humility to go to confession, but hearing a confession is often humbling for the priest himself! The priest does indeed kneel with the sinner as they both profess their hope in the Father of all mercies.

What is it like to hear confessions? It is not the sins that stand out (either in God's eyes or in the confessor's memory). What makes the lasting impression is the courage and humility of those turning to God as best they can so as to turn away from their sins.

THE ROLE OF THE CONFESSOR

Catholic tradition has often assigned the confessor the role of *judge*. The term is unpopular with many, as it conjures up distressing images of courtrooms, prosecuting attorneys, and prison sentences.

Yet there is another side to the notion of the confessor as judge—one I have experienced many times as a minister of the sacrament. The *Catechism* describes the confessor in this way:

Epilogue: Hearing Confession

> When he celebrates the sacrament of Penance, the priest is fulfilling the ministry of the Good Shepherd who seeks the lost sheep, of the Good Samaritan who binds up wounds, of the Father who awaits the prodigal son and welcomes him on his return, and of the just and impartial judge whose judgment is both just and merciful. The priest is the sign and the instrument of God's merciful love for the sinner. The confessor is not the master of God's forgiveness, but its servant. (1465–66)

The priest, the servant of God's forgiveness, is the "just and impartial judge." In that regard, the priest is not the agent of the prosecuting attorney, meticulously collecting all possible evidence so as to secure a verdict of "guilty as charged." Nor does he side with the unscrupulous defense attorney, seeking any and every loophole that would absolve one from taking responsibility for one's actions. The confessor as judge stands in a unique position—with his penitents, affirming their contrition *with* them and speaking God's word of peace *to* them. The priest is a judge like no other, a judge that both sympathizes and empathizes with those seeking forgiveness.

As a "judge," the priest acts to assure fairness in the confessional; not by ferreting out concealed sins, but by assisting penitents as they accuse themselves—and by assisting them *with their own defense*. Many times the priest acts as judge simply by allowing "the other side" of the person to speak: by allowing a penitent's contrition and sorrow to speak alongside his or her accusation of sin. He assures that the sacrament has a defense as well, so that the Father's voice of forgiveness is not drowned out by a penitent's feelings of hopelessness and despair.

CONTRITION VERSUS PERFECTION

"I know I'm going to make the same mistakes and commit the same sins. Why keep going to confession?" Three decades of hearing confessions have taught me that, while some penitents may tire of confessing the same sins, God never tires of offering them his saving grace.

The ticket for admittance to the confessional is contrition, not perfection. We celebrate the sacrament not by promising impeccable, sinless behavior in the future, but by pledging to do better, and to forgive as we are forgiven.

That we are forgiven, even without being able to promise God or ourselves a sinless future, is but the miracle of God's love, a love that seeks us out even before we ask for it. Remember what the parable of the prodigal son teaches us (Luke 15:11–32). The father did not just happen to casually glance out the window and see his younger son returning home. He was waiting for him, ever vigilant, ever ready to meet him with a loving embrace.

We should not avoid the sacrament because we can't always say "no" to our sin; we should seek reconciliation because we can never afford to say "no" to God's grace. Let us remember Jesus' call to peace: "Come to me, all who labor and are heavy laden, and I will give you rest" (Matt 11:28).

God invites us to approach him, not because we have earned the right to do so, but because we need the invitation to draw near. Such an invitation is offered us in and in spite of our sin, and not only if and after we have reached perfection. We do not confess the same sins over and over because we need to remind ourselves (or God) of our repeated failings; we confess them because they are part of our life—but not nearly as important a part as is God's merciful love and forgiveness. *And we need to remind ourselves of that!*

Epilogue: Hearing Confession

COME IN HOPE, GO IN PEACE

I remember those grade school confessions years ago. I remember examining my conscience. I remember trying not to be afraid. I remember trying at least not to act afraid!

I also remember wondering what it was like to be the priest. What would it be like to hear confessions, to pronounce God's forgiveness, to minister to those who admit their sins? As my teachers insisted, it is not being scandalized, but neither is it, as described by some, the most boring job in the world.

To hear confessions is to be impressed by the sincerity, humility, and determination of so many who know they have sinned—but who strive to do better, and who call on the grace of God to assist them in their struggle. To hear confessions is to be humbled, for it is indeed humbling to witness in others an uncommon honesty, a tender love, a responsive conscience. To be minister of the sacrament is to act as a judge who assures that this sacrament is "a tribunal of mercy rather than of strict and rigorous justice" (*Reconciliation and Penance* 31).

NOTES

CHAPTER ONE

1. The *Catechism* is quoting here from the Second Vatican Council's *Dogmatic Constitution on the Church* (*Lumen gentium*) 11, §2.

2. The *Catechism* (2089) defines apostasy as the total repudiation of the Christian faith.

3. The late Pope John Paul II, in his 1984 *Reconciliation and Penance* (17), drew upon one of the Church's greatest theologians and distinguished between mortal and venial sin in this way:

> According to St. Thomas [Aquinas, d. 1274], in order to live spiritually man must remain in communion with the supreme principle of life, which is God, since God is the ultimate end of man's being and acting. Now sin is a disorder perpetrated by the human being against this life-principle. And when through sin, the soul commits a disorder that reaches the point of turning away from its ultimate end God to which it is bound by charity, then the sin is mortal; on the other hand, whenever the disorder does not reach the point of a turning away from God, the sin is venial. For this reason venial sin does not deprive the sinner of sanctifying grace, friendship with God, charity and therefore eternal happiness, whereas just such a deprivation is precisely the consequence of mortal sin. Furthermore, when sin is considered from the point of view of the punishment it merits, for St. Thomas and other doctors, mortal sin is the sin which, if unforgiven, leads

to eternal punishment; whereas venial sin is the sin that merits merely temporal punishment (that is, a partial punishment which can be expiated on earth or in purgatory).

4. The canon continues: "Only physical or moral impossibility excuses from confession of this type; in such a case reconciliation can be obtained by other means." We will look at the canon in full later.

5. Sacramental words of absolution said by the priest, *Rite of Penance* 46; *Catechism* 1449.

CHAPTER TWO

1. Quoting from the sixteenth-century Council of Trent, the *Rite of Penance* 7a, states: "To obtain the saving remedy of the sacrament of penance, according to the plan of our merciful God, the faithful must confess to a priest each and every grave sin that they remember after an examination of conscience."

2. The text continues: "These will underline the fact that sin and its forgiveness have a social aspect."

CHAPTER THREE

1. Italics in the original.
2. *Catechism* 2477:

Respect for the reputation of persons forbids every attitude and word likely to cause them unjust injury. He becomes guilty:

—of *rash judgment* who, even tacitly, assumes as true, without sufficient foundation, the moral fault of a neighbor;

—of *detraction* who, without objectively valid reason, discloses another's faults and failings to persons who did not know them;

—of *calumny* who, by remarks contrary to the truth, harms the reputation of others and gives occasion for false judgments concerning them.

CHAPTER FOUR

1. The document "*Vademecum* [Companion] for Confessors Concerning Some Aspects of the Morality of Conjugal Life" is a guide for confessors. It was published by the Pontifical Council for the Family in 1997.

2. A tragic example with which my readers will be familiar would be the situation of United 93, the hijacked flight on 9/11 on which the passengers, knowing their deaths were likely, spent their last minutes attempting to regain control of the aircraft.

3. Many canon lawyers understand "a long time" as about a month.

4. *Code of Canon Law*:

> Can. 961 §1. Absolution cannot be imparted in a general manner to many penitents at once without previous individual confession unless: 1. danger of death is imminent and there is insufficient time for the priest or priests to hear the confessions of the individual penitents; 2. there is grave necessity, that is, when in view of the number of penitents, there are not enough confessors available to hear the confessions of individuals properly within a suitable period of time in such a way that the penitents are forced to be deprived for a long while of sacramental grace or holy communion through no fault of their own. Sufficient necessity is not considered to exist when confessors cannot be present due only to the large number of penitents such as can occur on some great feast or pilgrimage.
>
> §2. It belongs to the diocesan bishop to judge whether the conditions required according to the norm of §1, n. 2 are present. He can determine the cases of such necessity, attentive to the criteria agreed upon with the other members of the conference of bishops.
>
> Can. 962 §1. For a member of the Christian faithful validly to receive sacramental absolution given to many at one time, it is required not only that the person is properly

disposed but also at the same time intends to confess within a suitable period of time each grave sin which at the present time cannot be so confessed.

§2. Insofar as it can be done even on the occasion of the reception of general absolution, the Christian faithful are to be instructed about the requirements of the norm of §1. An exhortation that each person take care to make an act of contrition is to precede general absolution even in the case of danger of death, if there is time.

Can. 963 Without prejudice to the obligation mentioned in can. 989, a person whose grave sins are remitted by general absolution is to approach individual confession as soon as possible, given the opportunity, before receiving another general absolution, unless a just cause intervenes.

5. "A person who is conscious of grave sin is not to...receive the body of the Lord without previous sacramental confession unless there is a grave reason and there is no opportunity to confess; in this case the person is to remember the obligation to make an act of perfect contrition which includes the resolution of confessing as soon as possible."

6. "Individual and integral confession and absolution constitute the only ordinary means by which a member of the faithful conscious of grave sin is reconciled with God and the Church. Only physical or moral impossibility excuses from confession of this type; in such a case reconciliation can be obtained by other means."

7. John M. Huels, *The Pastoral Companion: A Canon Law Handbook for Catholic Ministry*, 4th updated ed. rev. (Montreal: Wilson & Lafleur Ltée, 2009), 147.

8. This is from *Baltimore Catechism* No. 3, published by Benzinger Brothers in 1949, questions 729–30 taken from the Web site: www.ourladyswarriors.org/faith/bc3-17.

9. Concerning excommunication, the *Catechism* 1463 states: "Certain particularly grave sins incur excommunication, the most severe ecclesiastical penalty, which impedes the reception of the sacraments and exercise of certain ecclesiastical acts, and for which absolu-

tion consequently cannot be granted, according to canon law, except by the Pope, the bishop of the place or priests authorized by them." The *Catechism* 2089 distinguishes among the sins of apostasy, heresy, and schism in this way: "*Heresy* is the obstinate post-baptismal denial of some truth which must be believed with divine and catholic faith, or it is likewise an obstinate doubt concerning the same; *apostasy* is the total repudiation of the Christian faith; *schism* is the refusal of submission to the Roman Pontiff or of communion with the members of the Church subject to him."

10. Whether an excommunication was incurred involves some complexities of canon law, and is a matter best left to your priest. The point I stress here is that one's (often incorrect or incomplete) understanding of excommunication should not keep one from approaching the confessional and your priest.

FURTHER RESOURCES

Various editions of the *Rite of Penance*, the *Catechism of the Catholic Church*, and the *Code of Canon Law* are available online and from most Catholic book stores.

www.usccb.org. The home page of the United States Conference of Catholic Bishops.

Saint John Paul II, *Apostolic Exhortation: Reconciliation and Penance*, 1984; http://www.vatican.va/holy_father/john_paul_ii/apost_ex hortations/documents/hf_jp-ii_exh_02121984_reconciliatio-et-paenitentia_en.html. An apostolic exhortation on humankind's need to "reconcile and be reconciled." Parts I and II offer an extensive reflection on conversion, reconciliation, and the mysteries of sin and forgiveness. Part III reviews Church teaching on the sacrament of reconciliation and offers Pope John Paul's insights and directives concerning its pastoral practice.

Pontifical Council for the Family, *Vademecum for Confessors Concerning Some Aspects of the Morality of Conjugal Life*, 1997; http://www.vatican.va/roman_curia/pontifical_councils/family/documents/rc_pc_family_doc_12021997_vademecum_en.html. Written as a "companion" for confessors, this document "offers a reference point for married penitents so that they can draw ever greater advantage from the practice of the sacrament of Reconciliation, and live their vocation to responsible parenthood in keeping with divine law, authoritatively taught by the Church. It will also serve as an aid for those who are preparing for marriage" (from the document's Introduction, 1).

A Confessor's Handbook
Revised and Expanded Edition
Kurt Stasiak, OSB

A guide filled with practical, straightforward advice, examples, and suggestions on how a confessor might celebrate the sacrament of reconciliation more effectively with his parishioners.

978-0-8091-4675-8　Paperback

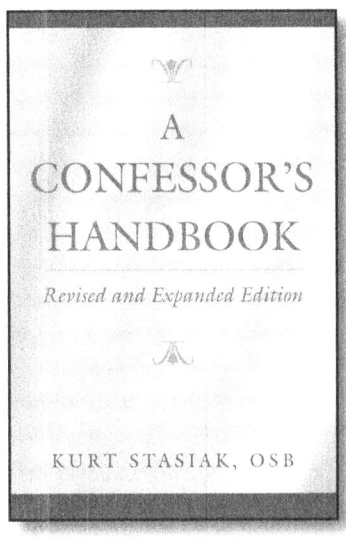

Healing God's People
Theological and Pastoral Approaches;
A Reconciliation Reader

Edited by Thomas A. Kane, CSP

Prominent theologians, mostly from the faculty at Boston College and its School of Theology, contribute essays to this collection on reconciliation.

978-0-8091-4822-6 Paperback

Cornerstones of Faith
Reconciliation, Eucharist, and Stewardship
Thomas Cardinal Collins

Thomas Cardinal Collins addresses fundamental elements of the life of Christian discipleship—reconciliation, eucharist, and stewardship—in this collection of three pastoral letters, from his tenure as Archbishop of Edmonton.

978-0-8091-4840-0   Paperback

The Future of the Sacrament of Penance

Frank O'Loughlin

Calls for a change in attitude toward, and a renewal in, understanding the use of the sacrament of penance.

978-0-8091-4556-0   Paperback

101 Questions & Answers on the Sacraments of Healing
Penance and Anointing of the Sick

Paul Jerome Keller, OP

This book is aimed at the general reader who desires insight into the Catholic teaching on the sacraments of penance and anointing; it addresses the theology of these two sacraments as well as particular concerns that both lay person and priest may have about them.

978-0-8091-4660-4   Paperback

Child's Guide to Reconciliation
Elizabeth Ficocelli

A colorful guide for children on receiving the sacrament of Reconciliation for the first time. Describes the purpose and procedure of the rite and helps children approach the sacrament with true comfort and a sense of joy. Ages 5-9.

0-8091-6709-3 Hardcover

Mercy
The Essence of the Gospel and the Key to Christian Life
Cardinal Walter Kasper

"This book has done me so much good." —Pope Francis

From one of the leading intellects in the Church today—one whom Pope Francis has described as a "superb theologian"—comes perhaps his most important book yet. Compassionate, bold, and brilliant, Cardinal Kasper has written a book which will be studied for generations.

978-0-8091-0609-7   Hardcover

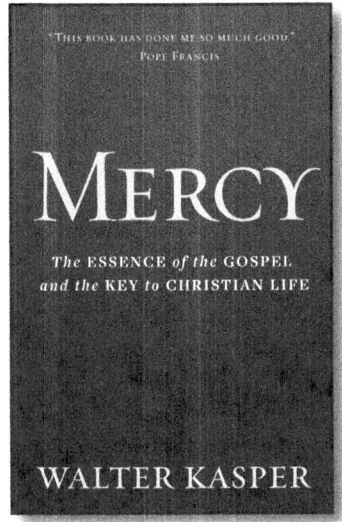

The Gospel of the Family
Cardinal Walter Kasper

Cardinal Kasper, in an address to the consistory, published in English exclusively by Paulist Press, advocates a stronger appreciation of marriage and the family—even on sensitive issues such as divorce and remarriage.

978-0-8091-4908-7   Paperback

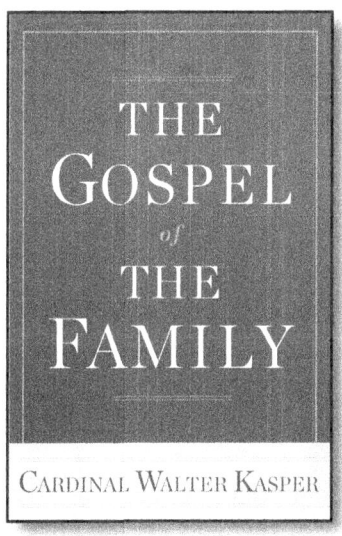

A Year with Pope Francis
Daily Reflections from His Writings
Edited by Alberto Rossa, CMF

This pocket-sized volume contains a treasure of reflections and quotations from beloved Pope Francis for each day of the year. These words from Pope Francis will strengthen you in faith, build you up in hope, and bring you closer to God.

978-0-8091-4889-9   Paperback

The Catholic Prayer Bible (NRSV)
Lectio Divina Edition
Paulist Press

An ideal Bible for anyone who desires to reflect on the individual stories and chapters of just one, or even all, of the biblical books, while being led to prayer through meditation on that biblical passage.

978-0-8091-0587-8   Hardcover
978-0-8091-4663-5   Paperback
978-0-8091-4766-3   Deluxe Edition

Where the Hell Is God?
*Richard Leonard, SJ;
foreword by James Martin, SJ*

Combines professional insights along with the author's own experience and insights to speculate on how believers can make sense of their Christian faith when confronted with tragedy and suffering.

978-1-58768-060-1 Paperback
978-0-8091-4749-6 Large Print Edition

Why Bother Praying?
Richard Leonard, SJ

Written by the bestselling author of Where the Hell Is God?, this accessible volume is for everyone who wonders how to pray, everyone who wonders what happens when you pray, and everyone who wonders if God hears our prayers.

978-0-8091-4803-5 Paperback